God in the ICU

DAVE WALKER MD

God in the **ICU**
by Dave Walker
Copyright © 2012
All rights reserved.

ISBN 9781466440319

When Dave Walker suffered a series of tragedies in his life, his faith in a loving God plummeted.

He decided to live for himself, since God did not appear to be interested. Despite a successful career as an anaesthetist with a special interest in Intensive Care, however, life lost its meaning. When in desperation he sought God with all his heart, God showed up and he started praying with his patients. Suddenly his life changed as he saw God intervene in response to prayer.

Set, first in a South Africa transitioning from oppression and armed struggle to reconciliation and democracy and then moving to the Middle East, **God in the ICU** takes you into the life of a doctor searching for more than just physical healing for his patients. From miraculous cure to comfort in the midst of suffering, his patients in ICU started to experience God while he faced his own personal trials that kept him seeking a God that he did not understand, but was learning to know more and more personally.

Foreword

The Intensive Care Unit is a special place in a hospital where the care is more complicated and demanding than almost any other part of the hospital. The ratio of staff to patient is high and most patients recover well but the risks are higher. The challenge to the doctors and the nurses is to monitor the patients well and make sure they recover quickly. With such critically ill patients and such a lot of genuine care, God is there in a special way.

I worked with Dave Walker for 15 years during which time he looked after my patients in the Intensive Care Unit, after having given the anaesthetic. Sometimes the operation lasted 6 to 12 hours and Dave was there for the full time and then still took over in the Intensive Care Unit for a full recovery.

Dave often said a prayer with the patient, if he could, and that created an atmosphere of faith and belief in the love of God. That was special. The patients appreciated it and I loved it. In that way the operation and the recovery were blessed by God. It was as if He was there with us as part of our team.

God in the ICU is the story of Dave's search for God and finding Him. Dave found God and found Him abundantly. He lived his faith to the full and shared it with patients and their families in the ICU.

Dave takes us on a Doctor's journey in his approach to the most ill patients. He shares with us his compassion. That is so moving. The *Art of Medicine* is to cure.

Here we read stories of how that happens. We share the concerns, the challenges of sickness and we experience, with Dave, the joys of healing.

From the beginning of the book the stories are moving, and a box of tissues is a help!

Dr Wolfgang Losken
Clinical Affiliated Professor, Plastic Surgery. University of North
Carolina.

Acknowledgements

This book would not have been possible without the loving support of so many people who have encouraged and helped me.

Firstly, Margie, my wife, endured endless conversations about just one subject – my book – and read numerous drafts always with constructive comments.

My three daughters Mandy, Dee and Tracey were always very enthusiastic about the chapters that I sent them to read and kept me going when doubts assailed me about my capabilities to finish the job.

Anne Erikson, my editor, is a gem. She went beyond a mere professional interest in the way she helped. Throughout the process I felt as if I had a friend helping me to hone and refine and clarify. Thank you, Anne.

Thank you, Timothy Sparks for proof reading and 'fine tuning' my book.

Then my friends, particularly Dave Ball (an enthusiast and great encourager), Garth Lee, Dave Shepherd, Richard Anderson, and Sonya Hunt all patiently read portions of the book and contributed to its final form with their comments and interest.

Lastly I wish to express my gratitude to God, who led me to start this book in the first place and, through His constant involvement in my life, has given me something to write about – in fact, something to sing about for the rest of my days.

Chapter One

A SENSE of DESTINY

"Hey God, can You hear me?"

    The shrill, triumphant voice of a six-year- old boy pierced the morning air from a treetop.

I had climbed to the summit of the Jacaranda tree in our garden and was savouring the victory. The ground was dizzyingly far below me and I felt sure that the top of the world could not be far off. And of course, I was close to heaven and therefore close to God.

I do not think that there was ever a time in my life when I doubted the existence of God. I remember at the questioning age of adolescence, when one thinks about things more intently, and questions everything; I was at a camp in the Zimbabwean bush. I had looked around at the flat-topped thorn trees providing shade for our tents and the tall Bauhinias, whose leaves fluttered in the wind like butterflies; I had listened to the ku-kurrrrrrr of the doves overhead and seen a timid bushbuck dart through our camp; I had observed the sensitive, complex ecosystem – everything designed to harmonise and sustain life in a slow, purposeful rhythm of seasons and I had settled the question once and for all. This could not have happened by accident: God was there.

    This is the tale of how He took my hand and led me down the path appointed for me, to show me the way in which He responds to our prayers and demonstrates His love in all manner of situations.

The story starts in 1940 in a simply furnished prefabricated house, nestled, with four others like it, amongst Msasa trees and tawny grass in a remote part of Zimbabwe overlooking the Umniati River. It was home to the engineer who supervised the power station. His young wife was looking anxiously at their newborn baby. He had not been well for two days, but today he looked worse. Instead of crying fretfully he was drowsy and listless and could not take the breast.

She glanced at her husband beside her. *"We need to get him to the hospital, Jack. I'm worried."* It was a three-hour bumpy ride in their old truck along a bush track to Kwe Kwe, the nearest town, and to the anxious parents each minute crawled by as their child lay still and pale beside them. They rushed into the Casualty Department, anxiously presenting the little bundle to the staff. After his examination, the doctor was abrupt.

"Why did you leave it so late? Your baby has malaria. There is no chance to save him now. He is going to die!"

Without even sterilising the skin, he plunged a needle into the little buttock, administering a massive dose of quinine, more as a token of treatment than with any true hope.

In anguish and guilt after the doctor's comment, the mother and father kept an anxious all-night vigil over their baby. Remarkably, the next day he had

improved, and although he developed an abscess from the quinine injection and pneumonia as a complication, he survived.

That was my introduction into this world. When I was old enough to understand, and heard them recall the story, it engendered in me a sense of destiny. God had spared me for a purpose. From the age of seven I knew I wanted to fulfil that destiny in the field of medicine and everything was assessed in terms of how it would help me to become a doctor. I devoured stories of doctors of compassion such as Dr Paul Brand, a Christian surgeon who worked amongst lepers, transforming their lives by making groundbreaking discoveries of the cause of their deformities and devising operations to counter their disabilities. I thrilled to tales of humanitarians such as Albert Schweitzer, a famous musician who then studied medicine and went on to found a mission station in Lambaréné, in the former French Equatorial Africa (now Gabon). And Taylor Caldwell's *Dear and Glorious Physician,* a novel about St Luke, the doctor disciple of Jesus, set my heart aflame as I dreamed, romantically, of the healing role I could play in society.

I somehow never doubted that I would be accepted for Medical School, but it was nevertheless a thrill as I set off on a three-day car journey from Zimbabwe to the University of Cape Town.

My time at Medical School came at a pivotal time in South Africa's history. On 21 March 1960, one year after my enrolment, a group of 20 000 unarmed people gathered at the police station in Sharpeville (a township near Vereeniging), to protest against laws which required every Black person to carry a 'pass'. The handful of police, confronted with such a large number of people, panicked and fired live ammunition into the crowd, massacring 69 people including women and children. Those were tense days in the history of the country and I have a vivid memory of an endless line of thousands upon thousands of Black people marching solemnly along De Waal Drive, the main highway into Cape Town, led by a young lawyer named Nelson Mandela. They were protesting the Sharpeville massacre and demanding compensation.

In response the South African Government passed a bill indemnifying the government retrospectively from responsibility for any such compensation. So, in my third year at Medical School, the *African National Congress* turned peaceful opposition into an armed struggle, and we lived in a declared State of Emergency.

In that atmosphere of secret government atrocities and acts of sabotage by *Umkhonte we Sizwe*, the military wing of the African National Congress, I was accumulating knowledge that I hoped would set me on a different course of compassion and healing.

At last the day arrived. The results of the final examination were pinned up and, pushing through the crowd and craning my neck, I saw my name on the list. I rushed to my excited parents to be greeted by my dad, for the first time, by my new title, *"Hello, Doc!"*

It felt so good! I was fulfilling my destiny.
During my time at Medical School I had fallen in love with a beautiful nurse and Penny and I were married two days after I graduated. Our honeymoon was spent travelling back to Zimbabwe so that I could commence my internship at Harare Hospital.
My introduction to medical practice was dramatic. I waited nervously for the phone to ring on my first night on call and jumped apprehensively at the shrill ring. I answered quickly, *"Hello."*

"Hello Dr Walker. Could you come to Casualty immediately: we have a child here whose arm has been bitten off by a crocodile!"

I raced to the Emergency Department to see a six-year-old boy lying on a trolley, the whites of his wide eyes shining against the black of his frightened little face. His right arm was missing, with the bone protruding through putrid flesh bloated with gas gangrene. This was a prelude to a hectic internship. With only four interns to manage a one thousand- bed hospital handling such dramatic cases, it was a baptism by fire. It was a time of busy days and gruelling nights, but we gained great experience very quickly.

And yet there was more...

During my time at Medical School I had become interested in anaesthesia. To see someone close their eyes and drift into unconsciousness in response to an injection was fascinating. I learned that it was the anaesthetist's responsibility to keep the body functioning as normally as possible while it was being assaulted by the strain of surgery and blood loss. The anaesthetic itself produces side effects and the anaesthetist must be aware of these and be ready to counteract them in the best possible way. Anaesthesia requires dexterity in placing intravenous, arterial, and epidural lines, a comprehensive knowledge of how the body functions normally and under surgery and a thorough understanding of drugs and how they work. The idea of using skill and knowledge to be the guardian of the patient, sheltering him through a major crisis in his life, had great appeal. Hence, I enrolled as a registrar in training in the Anaesthetic Department at Groote Schuur Hospital in Cape Town.

Chapter Two

HISTORY in the MAKING

My training at Groote Schuur, a teaching hospital, came easily and intuitively. I loved it. One incident remains etched in my memory like a highlighted script in the play of my life. The date was 3 December 1967. I had been a registrar in training for just ten months.

The shrill ring of the telephone interrupted my thoughts as I browsed through a magazine in the duty room of the Anaesthetic Department. It was nine in the evening and my night on call had started quietly. I picked up the receiver. Even without any introduction there was no mistaking the high- pitched strident voice with an Afrikaans accent characteristic of the Northern Cape. He rolled his

'rrrs' as he spoke:

"Now look! It's all verry well everryone talking about a heart trransplant, but nobody is coming to rresuscitate the donorr!"

It was the distinctive voice of Chris Barnard! *"Oh! You want me to resuscitate the donor?" "Yes, of course!"* The phone slammed down. My heart missed a beat. I had heard a vague rumour that Chris was going to attempt a heart transplant, but I was unaware of any activity that night. I rushed to the cardiac wards and there, in and out of a single ward, like bees around a honey pot, were the elite of the cardiac team.

I must have looked as startled as I felt as I entered the room. There were people putting up intravenous and arterial lines, drawing up drugs, taking measurements, recording, issuing orders. ...What was there for me, a young trainee anaesthetist, to do? The neurosurgical professor approached me.

"Don't worry about any cardiac resuscitation. Just look after her breathing."

Relieved, I moved quickly to the head of the bed, placed a tube into the windpipe of the young girl, the victim of a horrific car accident. I attached her to a ventilator, forcing oxygen into her lungs to keep her heart functioning.

Within a few minutes, Dr Ozinsky, the cardiac anaesthetist, arrived. As he took over the care of the donor I went to the operating theatre. There I scrubbed and gowned and began to draw up the anaesthetic drugs that would, or might be, required.

Unfortunately, as the procedure got underway, I was called away to another emergency in a nearby theatre. I could not participate, save every now and again, when I could get someone to look after my patient while I popped in to look.

Even in our theatre the atmosphere was electric as the reports came back.

The whine of a saw told us the donor's chest was being opened and her heart removed. Today things are far more controlled than in those pioneering days. Then, the heart was removed from the donor at the same time as the operation on the recipient and carried across to the recipient's surgical team in a nearby theatre.

Then came the news: *"Washkansky's heart is out!"*

During open heart surgery the patient is cooled down so that the organs require less oxygen. Below a certain temperature the heart stops. Often, as the patient is re-warmed at the end of the operation, it requires a small shock to kick-start the heart again.

"He is sewing in the heart."

History was being made. The heart, mystically associated from the beginning of time with the very essence of a person, was being given as a gift of life to a dying man. Would it work? Was it, after all, only a beautiful, intricate pump?

"The heart is in. They are re-warming the patient."

We were all mentally holding our breath. Would it start beating? Then a loud cheer erupted that could be heard in my theatre. With just two small shocks, the heart of a young girl started beating in Louis Washkansky's body. I felt as if I had been peripherally involved in a miracle.

The operation finished as the dawn rays fingered the Cape sky. Breakfast was arranged in the theatre coffee room and, with an air of excitement, everyone was shaking Chris Barnard by the hand, congratulating him, and wondering for how long the news would be on the headlines in the papers. We little realised that it would reverberate around the world for weeks and months, capturing the admiration of scientists, and the wonder of the public.

Throughout the city of Cape Town, now suddenly famous, one heard virtually no other subject spoken about for weeks. The Coloured community, renowned for their sense of humour, entered enthusiastically into the celebration. Shortly after the transplant, a man, lying unconscious and very still and with alcohol on his breath, was brought into the Emergency Room. He was so motionless that it was alarming, but the doctor could find nothing wrong. He was puzzled. Was he just very drunk? Was he feigning unconsciousness? Or was there something more serious? The doctor called in a colleague and they stood beside the trolley discussing him. Suddenly, without warning, the patient's eyes blinked wide open, he sat bolt upright before the startled doctors, put his hand across his chest and said, *"Gimmee a new heart, Doc!"* Then he promptly sank back on the trolley simulating a coma once more.

Other patients were more nervous and suspicious of the motives of the surgeons, making us promise that we would not take out their heart while we were operating on them!

And all the while, with a sense of fulfilling my destiny, I was accumulating knowledge and expertise, not without a lot of fun on the way.

Anaesthetics are a little different these days, with patients arousing much more quickly and more clear-headed. Sometimes, in those days, we would have unpredictable reactions from the patients as they emerged from the anaesthetic. One burly man started sobbing uncontrollably as he was waking up from a minor operation. Worried that he had perhaps experienced something during the procedure, I apprehensively asked him what was wrong.

"Seven years." He bawled, *"I nursed her for seven years. Seven whole years before she died!"*

Concerned at his grief I asked him who this was.

"It was my aunt," he snorted and snivelled as the tears rolled down his face.

I was impressed that he was so attached to his aunt as to be so upset and told him so.

"No, you don't understand! I nursed her for seven years and when she died, she left all her fortune to a home for cats!"

He was becoming a little more coherent as he sobbed the anaesthetic out of his system and I questioned him more about his distress. It was not a fortune, but he would have liked it and he felt that he had deserved it. I sympathised with him and asked him when this had happened. To my astonishment, he told me it had happened fifteen years ago! And, as the anaesthetic revealed, he was still smarting!

The specialist examinations were sat in two parts. The first part tested the foundation knowledge required to give an anaesthetic and the final examination was a test of one's expertise.

I successfully passed the first part, but before I could sit the second part, an opportunity arose that I seized with both hands. A post as Medical Officer became vacant at Oranjemund, a diamond mining town on the edge of the Namib Desert in Namibia. My spirit of adventure rose. I applied for the post and was successful.

Chapter Three

EXCITEMENT, TRAGEDY and QUESTIONS

As Penny and I and our little blonde two-year- old daughter set off in our rattling Austin I had a sense of excitement and apprehension. This was new territory for me. We arrived at the vast Orange River – the border between the Republic of South Africa and Namibia – and were greeted by a friendly mining official. He pointed to a long row of garages lining the side of the river.

"Park your car in number 86. We'll come and pick you up from there."

Obediently I drove my car to garage 86 and within a minute a man in a large 4 x 4 took our luggage and ushered us into his vehicle. We drove across the bridge and into the town, where he deposited us outside a charming little mine house.

I had started the experience of living in a 'closed' town. Because there was a constant temptation to smuggle uncut diamonds out of the town, it was 'closed'. On entering, anything that could be used to secrete diamonds, such as my car, had to be left outside. Alternatively, it could be brought in, but then it would never be allowed out again. In addition, all personnel entering or leaving passed through a tight security check. On exiting, they and their luggage were X-rayed to ensure they had not swallowed diamonds or hidden them elsewhere. Long before it became routine practice at airports, our radiologist at the hospital joked that on his curriculum vitae he could put, *"Have X-rayed 10 000 suitcases!"*

Life was a whirl of activity when we arrived. Amid all the formalities of signing on and becoming accustomed to the hospital, the manager arranged a party to welcome us. The mining parties had a reputation for being lavish and wild and ours lived up to that. There was hilarity and dancing and the liquor was flowing freely. I had had more than my share of alcohol and was laughing and joking with my wife and the engineers when someone tapped me on the shoulder. *"There is a telephone call for you, Dave."*

As I picked up the receiver, I was curious. Who would even know that I was here, let alone phone me at eleven in the evening?

"Dave!" The voice of Erica, my brother's wife, sounded thin and small.

"Yes, what's wrong?" The fun of the party was still with me and I was not taking her too seriously.

"Dave, Ray has been in a car accident."

My fun-loving brother! He seemed to be accident prone. Less than a year ago he had borrowed my car and returned it with a bad dent down the side.

"Sorry to hear that, Erica. Is the car badly damaged? Is Ray hurt?"

Her voice was even smaller and the words, barely audible, fought their way out from a tight throat. *"He is very bad, Dave. They don't expect him to survive the night."*

My world changed! Ray and I were very close. Often, as one of us was thinking something, with an uncanny understanding, the other would speak the thought. We even looked so alike that we were frequently mistaken for one other. Ray dying?! My head was spinning with the alcohol I had consumed. I struggled to clear my thoughts and come to grips with what I had heard.

"Are you sure? Is that what the doctors say? Where is he? Who is his doctor?" I knew all the doctors at Groote Schuur Hospital.

"It was a terrible accident, Dave. He is in the neurosurgery ward at Groote Schuur."

"I will get back to you in the morning, Erica. I will try to fly

to Cape Town as quickly as possible."

A phone call to the neurosurgeon confirmed it. Ray, not wearing a seat belt and travelling fast in pouring rain, had hit a concrete pillar. As his head crashed against the windscreen, shattering his skull, so his chest was flung against the steering wheel, bruising his heart and splintering his ribs, which tore into his lungs. He could not survive.

With a numb sense of unreality, we caught the flight to Cape Town the following morning. I identified my dead brother and then with Erica (his pregnant wife of just three months), my grieving parents and my sister, we buried him.

I went back to work, but every so often, as if from nowhere, intense sorrow would breach the surface, my eyes filling with tears. For three weeks I thought that I would tear apart from grief as waves of agonising sadness gripped my heart.

Then that was replaced by a cold anger against God. How could He have let this happen? Although I was not sure whether He was personal or some kind of 'Force for Good' I had always regarded Him as loving and caring. He could have stopped this happening. Didn't He hold the whole world in His hands? Is that how He treated His creation? My view of Him changed. I lost my sense of security in His love. It appeared as if He just looked on from afar and let us get on with our own lives. All right! Then that is what I would do. Gone was my sense of destiny. From now on I would work for excellence for myself alone.

And I enjoyed it. Oranjemund was certainly different from the severe academic world of the Anaesthetic Department of Groote Schuur Hospital. Looking back, little scenes, like video clips, play across my mind. ...

On the mine there was no veterinarian. The pharmacist had taken an interest in veterinary science, and now here I was with a knowledge of anaesthetics, so I was seconded to be the veterinary anaesthetist. When an animal needed to be neutered or spayed, I gave the anaesthetic and the pharmacist removed the offending organs. One day a basset-hound which had dislocated its jaw was brought in by its owners. A comical dog at best, the animal, with his mouth open and his lower jaw at an angle, looked like a quaint, wrinkled Texan that got stuck halfway through a side-of-the-mouth *"Howdy!"*

My standard technique for giving a dog an anaesthetic was to soak a wad of cotton wool in anaesthetic vapour and hold it over his nose and mouth. Eventually the dog would topple over and the operation could commence. For the basset I had an enormous wad of cotton wool which I doused liberally with the vapour and attempted to get him to breathe it in. Every time I tried to wrap it around his open, skew mouth, however, he slobbered over it, effectively sealing off the anaesthetic, which came back at me. Soon both the pharmacist and I were giggling and light-headed while the basset, still on his feet, gave us mournful, disapproving looks. I changed my plan and gave him intravenous Pentothal which felled him like a bullet. But it was a struggle to reduce the dislocation of his jaw and I needed to give him more and more anaesthetic.

Finally, with a click the pharmacist 'vet' got the jaw back and I waited for the anaesthetic to wear off as the dog lay on the table. I waited and waited. Four hours later the sleeping dog became something of a phenomenon at the hospital. Finally, after six hours, as the hospital was closing for the night, he raised a bleary eye, pulled himself up on his short legs, shook his head and fell over. Then, weaving dangerously, he staggered home with his relieved owners.

My mind's video clip changes to a portly, affable man who was so devoted to his wife that when she went into labour, the doctor had to book him into a bed beside her. As she groaned with a contraction, so he held his stomach and writhed on his bed crying out with sympathetic pain. They had two children. I think after that he persuaded his wife that that was all the labour he could take!

On the mine there were from time to time attempts to smuggle uncut diamonds out of the town. In a Hollywood-style sting operation the helicopter pilot was caught, dismissed, and escorted out of the closed town within twenty-four hours.

The Ovambo workers, who swept the mine floor and picked up diamonds by hand, were the most tempted. They were searched at the end of every day and subjected to a rollcall and curfew in the evening. During one dramatic long weekend, one of the workers hid an unknown number of diamonds, feigned sick and registered at Sick Bay. He managed to deceive the residence staff into thinking that he was in Sick Bay and the Sick Bay staff into thinking that he had recovered and was in the hostel. Thus, he escaped rollcall for three days. On the Monday morning a trail of footprints was discovered which led out of the residence and disappeared into the Namib Desert. The worker had chosen to take his treasure and tramp two hundred kilometres across scorching sands, enduring arid, mercilessly hot days and freezing-cold nights. He faced at least three days' trek without water. We never heard whether he made it or whether his bones still lie dry and windblown beside his illegal bounty.

In the meanwhile, Erica, my brother's widow, gave birth to their baby, a girl, whom she named Deirdre.

They both came to stay with us for a while and my heart broke to see her on her own, longing for her darling husband to be there to share with her the joy of their child. My heart broke for her and the baby and I lamented the loss of a God of love as it seemed, in my eyes, that He had been replaced by Someone impersonal who looked on from above without intervening.

However, I tried not to think too much about that and immersed myself instead in the fun life of a mining town   a sheltered existence of easy hours, plenty of sport and parties.

I wrote my final anaesthetic examination while I was there – a difficult thing to do outside of the academic environment of a teaching hospital. I did not expect to pass and so I offered everyone a champagne party if I did. To my delight I passed the first time. I heard that the party that we threw was still being talked about six months after we had left!

I had been in Oranjemund for eighteen months. Having passed my anaesthetic examination it was time to return to my first love. At the start of 1971 I was accepted back at Groote Schuur as a Consultant Anaesthetist.

Chapter Four

WRESTLING with GOD

Although I had enjoyed my interlude in Oranjemund, it was gratifying to be back in anaesthetics. I now had a teaching role, which meant that I was responsible for two or three operating rooms, supervising the registrars in training. I was in charge of anaesthetics for the Obstetrics and Gynaecology Department. Obstetrics is always a satisfying department in which to work. One has two patients to consider, as the work requires anaesthetizing the mother in a way that least affects the baby. Unlike most surgery, which often involves the loss of a part of one's body, obstetrics brings the gift of a new life as the little new-born, eyes blinking perplexedly at the first light, brings the promise of new hopes and dreams.

Part of my duty as a consultant was to teach the medical students. There can be few people more brash and cocksure than a newly qualified medical consultant. Full of newly-acquired knowledge, a Messianic sense of the healing power that that knowledge produces and a confidence as yet unmodified by any of the sobering failures that experience brings, many consultants strut around with puffed-up egos that just ask to be burst. As a medical student I had had the demeaning experience of being talked down to from the lofty self-images of these little gods. Now I was one of them! My deflator came in the form of a lovely patient.

I was teaching a group of medical students to give anaesthetics for minor gynaecological procedures. I allowed one student to give the injection to put the patient to sleep, another to hold the mask on the patient's face and others to take turns to regulate the flow of anaesthetic through the mask. In this case the patient was a beautiful girl with flowing blonde hair pouring over her shoulders and around her head onto the pillow. Seeking to impress the students, I was supervising them in a superior manner, showing them how to regulate the anaesthetic, to anticipate the end of the procedure and to turn the anaesthetic gas off just prior to the end so that the patient awoke promptly. Things went exactly to plan and as the operation finished the patient started stirring.

"You see," I said boastfully, *"that is just how it should work."*

With that the girl mumbled something. The students lined the operating table on either side as I bent my ear close to her lovely face and said, *"What did you say?"*

With her eyes still closed she tilted her beautiful head slightly to my ear and, to the students' delight said, in a seductive whisper that carried across the room, *"Kiss me!"* As she became more conscious, she apologized profusely; in her confused state she had thought I was her boyfriend. But the damage was done and my ego deflated!

One day, eight months into the post, as I was supervising two registrars in the gynaecology theatre, I was called to the phone. A man, in an official-sounding tone, spoke with a thick Afrikaans accent.

"Is that Dr David Walker?" *"Yes."*

"This is the South African Police. Are you related to Mrs Erica Walker?"

"Yes. Is something wrong?"

"We need you to come around to her residence right away."

"What has happened?"

"I am afraid I cannot tell you, sir. You need to come here."

"I am in the middle of giving an anaesthetic. Can it wait?"

"No, I'm sorry, sir, it cannot wait. You need to come urgently."

My mind was racing. Erica had brought her little daughter, Deirdre, to me over the weekend. She had a slight cold, but nothing to worry about – or so I thought. Had I missed something? Had there been some tragedy with Deirdre? Hastily I organised a replacement in the theatre and raced to Erica's house.

I was met on the porch by a burly policeman with a gentle, sympathetic manner. He led me into the house. There, lying on the carpet, like the tragic heroine in the finale of a dramatic opera, lay

Erica. She was on her side, her lower arm outstretched while her long brown tresses spilled onto the carpet from around her pale face. Beside her, a coffee cup lay on its side, the coffee staining the carpet in a dark splash as it had fallen to the ground. Her eyes were closed in death. The police had been called after the maid had had no answer to her knocking. They discovered Erica on the floor and Deirdre standing in her cot waiting for her mother. Near Erica was an unfinished letter to her cousin explaining excitedly that she had just been chosen to captain the Western Province Women's hockey team on tour. It appeared that she had felt unwell, got up, coffee cup in hand to fetch something, and collapsed. The autopsy revealed no cause of death.

It was most probably a sequel to playing strenuous sport with an influenza infection. We now know that such an infection can affect the heart and cause it to go out of rhythm, sometimes fatally. If a bad rhythm stops the heart, then there is no structural damage and so nothing abnormal is found on autopsy.

We faced the next two weeks in a blur of pain and frantic activity. With such grief everything was an effort and yet there was so much to do. Erica's heartbroken parents and sister moved like automatons as together we sorted through all her belongings. And, of course, there were many of Ray's possessions that she had held onto; piercing, poignant reminders to me of my loss. Family members took turns to look after Deirdre during that time.

Trying to make rational decisions through the crushing pain of it all, coming so soon after my brother's death, was overwhelming. At any time, waves of deep heaving sobs came unasked and uncontrollably from my heart that seemed about to burst with sorrow. Slowly the fog lifted enough for us to think a little more clearly.

Penny and I agreed that we would like to adopt Deirdre. She and our daughter, Mandy, had formed a firm friendship when Erica and Deidre visited us in Oranjemund, and this had continued on our return to Cape Town. Erica's family graciously concurred.

It was a difficult time, mourning for a sister-in-law whom we dearly loved and coping with a new child as our own, but slowly we settled into a new routine. I had always taken great delight in my little daughter, Mandy. Now I had another daughter to love as well. In a strange way my grief, though still there, was transmuted into a deep love for this vulnerable little seventeen-month-old child.

And yet through it all there was a kind of despair at God. He really did seem distant and uncaring. It appeared that we had to cope on our own in this imperfect world of apparently random pain and joy.

Back at work the Head of Department was kind to me and gave me easy shifts, slowly easing me into responsibility once more. Six months passed and we were settling into a routine. Deirdre was legally adopted and had become Mandy's shadow, following her and imitating her every move.

Then one evening, with the children safely tucked in bed, there was a knock on the door. We opened the door to Jack, Erica's dad. As we welcomed him in and offered him a seat, he took it hesitantly and distractedly.

"Is there something wrong, Jack?"

Jack was an enormously likeable man, always composed and in control; it was unlike him to look agitated.

"It's Joy," he said, biting his lip. *"She has cancer."*

Joy was his wife. She had been suffering from intermittent depression for a long time, but when it did not grip her, her bright eyes, framed in laughter lines, sparkled with personality and humour. For many years she had had a rattling smoker's cough, but recently it had become worse and she had been feeling unwell. A chest X-ray revealed lung cancer so extensive that there was nothing that could be done. She would die within a few months. The news hit me like a shock of cold water. Suddenly life seemed so fragile. First Ray, then Erica and now Joy in the space of just over two years.

I capitulated; I could not fight God. If He really cared I needed Him to come through in this situation. I had no idea how to talk to Him or to pray but I knew that the little Anglican Church that I passed on my way to work held a communion service daily at 6.00 am. I began attending that service every morning before I went to work to try to make contact with God. Looking back, that was my first experience of Him. Every time I took the bread and the wine, I felt a supernatural peace flood my being. But I resisted it. I did not want that. I did not just want comfort. I wanted Joy healed.

We watched with helpless emptiness as Joy lay dying. It was in the era (before the enlightening days of the Hospice movement), when patients were not told that they were dying. And so, we played games. Joy knew she was dying, and she knew that we knew, but no one said anything. Penny and I visited her regularly and watched as she deteriorated rapidly. Often, as I sat by Joy's bed when I thought she was sleeping, I would surreptitiously put my hand on the blanket over her knee and try to pray. Sometimes I thought I saw her peeping at me, but no one said anything because although both Joy and I knew she was dying, neither of us had disclosed this to the other.

Joy did not recover. I had tried. I had cried out to God and He had apparently ignored me. It seemed He made His decisions and they were unbending. There is a popular song, From a Distance, the final chorus of which so echoed my thoughts as it sings of how:

"...God is watching us from a distance. Oh, God is watching us, God is watching. God is watching us from a distance."

Back at work I felt restless. I still enjoyed it, but I did not enjoy life so much, so I decided to resign and to spend a year doing short-term work in the United Kingdom to try to get some direction in my life.

Chapter Five

RESTORATION

Although I had no work to go to in Oxford, a friend offered us a house there at a nominal rental.

The house in Cumnor Hill was more than we could have dreamed for. A wooden gate in a ranch fence festooned with climbing roses led into a garden of oak trees, conifers, and lawns. A path led to a formal white front door with a brass knocker. The back of the house looked down a sloping lawn lined with rose beds, to a wooded area which our little girls immediately and aptly named Bluebell Wood.

The time in Oxford was a time of restoration. Pert robins came to the bird feeder or hopped unafraid onto the windowsill; squirrels scampered busily from tree to tree; a family of foxes came regularly out of the wood to the lawn, the cubs stumbling awkwardly as they played; and rabbits hopped across the lawn and into the rose garden.

One night, when winter came, Penny shook me awake me at 2.00 am.

"Do you believe in Wonderland?" she whispered, and pulled me to the window.

It was snowing and there, in the moonlight, was a scene of such beauty it struck my heart with wonder. The conifers were draped with snow, the soft round edges tinged with moonlight; the bare oaks, their branches top-edged with snow, stood serene in a white blanket which covered the ground and transformed the bird feeder into a miniature white-thatched house. The reflections of distant streetlights glistened softly in the snow. All was still, save for the gently falling flakes. The cold, pale moonlight lit the scene with a surreal light as we sat at the window enthralled, our spirits stilled and united by the tranquil beauty.

I had managed to find a few weeks' work as a consultant covering the night shift at Banbury Hospital. It was not burdensome, and it meant that we were free during the day to explore the beautiful Cotswolds with their homely cottages made of their distinctive yellow Cotswold stone. It was good, consolidating family time. Following my easy time in Banbury came more demanding work at the prestigious Nuffield Orthopaedic Centre in Oxford.

Much of the work done there was joint replacement surgery. The theatres were specially constructed to avoid infection – devastating as a complication of new joint surgery. Three sides of the operating area were walled in thick glass, so that the surgeons operated within an enclosure. I anaesthetised the patient and positioned him through the open fourth side, which was then walled off by a sterile drape that hung from the top, over the patient's shoulders and down to the floor on either side of him. The operating team wore a sort of "space suit" which consisted of a sterile gown incorporating a closed helmet through which air was pumped for them to breathe. To communicate they had a microphone and earphone within the helmet. Their speech was broadcast to the rest of the surgical team and also through a loudspeaker to those of us who were outside the surgical enclosure. It was state of the art then, but has since been discarded.

Occasionally a trainee was caught out by the system. One such was a visiting American registrar who was assisting at a hip replacement operation. The chief surgeon was not happy with the way he was assisting and complained to him every few minutes. The trainee turned to the scrub sister and, in what was intended to be an aside, said to her, *"The old b@%*$* is in a really bad mood today."* His "aside" went through his microphone out into the whole theatre and also into the earphones of the old b@%*$,* doing nothing to improve his mood!

Each day I had a 60-minute drive home to Cumnor Hill from the hospital and it soon became the highlight of my day. The 'dreaming spires' of Oxford University, like good classical music, became sweeter to behold with each repetition. Each spire, so distinctive of the college it represented, nevertheless blended into harmony with its silhouetted fellows like the chords of a silent visual symphony linking heaven and earth.

While we were in Oxford, Penny gave birth to Tracey, a beautiful new daughter for us and a sister for Mandy and Deirdre. Our little family was now complete.

All too soon my post there ended, and I decided to return to South Africa. I was accepted for a post at Edendale Hospital in Pietermaritzburg. It had a good reputation and I wanted something different from Cape Town, with its memories of such loss.

So, one afternoon in February 1974, while the world was reeling from unprecedented oil hikes and a global recession, and Abba was wowing the world with their catchy songs and distinctive sound, our family of Penny, me and three little girls aged five, three and six months arrived at the door of an unpretentious flat in Pietermaritzburg, Kwa-Zulu Natal, ready to start a new chapter in our lives.

We spent the day unpacking. Then, as the sun set and it grew dark, I flicked the light switch. Nothing happened. We had forgotten to have our electricity turned on by the municipality. What were we to do with our small children? We could not cook, and they could not bath. I remembered a doctor friend who had worked with me at Groote Schuur and had moved to Pietermaritzburg. I phoned and explained our predicament to him, and he invited us over for supper and a bath!

As we enjoyed being in a South African home again and were reminiscing over supper with my colleague about Groote Schuur, he turned to me and surprised me with a question.

"So, what do you think of my letter?"

I was puzzled. I had never received a letter from him, but in what I deemed an extraordinary coincidence, he had written on behalf of the anaesthetists in his private practice, offering me a share in the partnership. I was completely unaware of the offer and yet here I was at his table. It was an attractive offer and I accepted, after serving some time at Edendale.

I have since come to see that this was no coincidence, but the hand of a loving God leading me. Though I had lost all faith in His love and was living for myself alone, He had not forgotten me. Private practice was where He was going to use me to show His true nature. As I started out, however, my disillusionment with God continued. I went to church occasionally, but it was with no sense of conviction of a personal, loving God. It merely seemed like a respectable thing to do.

Chapter Six

PRIVATE PRACTICE

I was apprehensive about entering private practice. I had always pictured myself involved with the less-privileged members of society and I did not like the idea of working with middle class patients and charging them for my services. To my surprise I discovered that it was c h a l l e n g i n g stimulating work and, in many ways, it was easier to provide a more holistic medical service when in private practice. I appreciated the efficiency of working with highly-trained, experienced colleagues using state-of-the art equipment.

I loved the fact that, unlike the state environment, where the patients might see a bewildering number of different doctors on their journey through the bureaucratic medical process, I was the only anaesthetist that the person would see for the preoperative assessment, the operation and the postoperative visit. I had time to build trust, to relate to the patient not just in terms of their illness, but to them as people, allowing them to express their fears, to ask questions, to tell me about their families. Then, when they came to the operating room, they already knew me – a familiar face in a foreign environment.

The concept of having a special ward to look after critically-ill patients – an Intensive Care Unit – was just over a decade old when I started private practice. I developed a keen interest in developing the ICU at Grey's Hospital in Pietermaritzburg where we worked, and soon had a reputation for anaesthetising major cases and looking after them in the ICU.

I also became the anaesthetist for the Pietermaritzburg Craniofacial Unit – the first of its kind in Southern Africa. The patients, most of whom were children, had gross deformities of their faces. Sometimes the central part of their face would be undeveloped, their lower jaw extending far beyond their front teeth and their eyes protruding wide and globular from shallow undeveloped sockets. At other times their eyes would sit as much as ten centimetres apart in a wide flat forehead on a triangular face, and at other times a wide slit would cleave the face from the palate right through the nose toward the eyes. The surgery was complex and required a whole team often working for several hours. The anaesthetic was also complicated and I enjoyed the challenge. We did not charge for the operations – our reward was to see patients transformed from monsters that were shunned by society to become at the very least acceptable, but often good-looking people, who could walk unnoticed down the street. Many of these children had been kept in a back room by their parents, hidden from society. Preoperatively, when one spoke to them, they would look down and away to the left or right, trying to hide their faces. To see them look you in the eye and smile confidently after their operation was a lasting joy. The Unit broke ground politically when, at the height of the apartheid era, permission was granted to look after patients of every race in a designated 'White' hospital.

It was not just surgical cases that I cared for in the ICU. Sometimes I would be asked to look after medical cases there, too. One such case was that of Ronnie, a bad asthmatic who had been involved in a car accident and broken both his legs. Ronnie had a complex personality. He was a big burly man with curly hair and an effeminate manner. He fussed about everything and had the nurses rolling their eyes as he asked yet again for them to adjust his bedclothes, then stir the sugar in his tea, or scratch an itchy spot on his back. He did not require an operation for his broken legs, but he had a pain threshold close to zero, so I inserted an epidural catheter (a plastic tube running next to his spine). Through this I could run local anaesthetic to provide pain relief for his legs. For three days he managed well, but then his asthma started to become much worse.

He sat propped up, arms extended, and shoulders hunched as he struggled to fill his wheezing lungs with oxygen. Words came two at a time between rasping breaths. *"You've ... got to... help me Doc! ... Do something ... I can't ... go on like this!"*

I agreed with him. The medication was not helping. He needed to be put on a ventilator to assist his breathing. I explained what was needed. I would give him a very quick anaesthetic, put a tube down his throat into his windpipe and keep him sedated while we helped his breathing. Despite my attempts at reassurance, he panicked at the thought and suddenly became very antagonistic.

"No, I... don't want that!"

He had a bell in his hand that he used constantly to summon the nurses. Now he lashed out at me with the bell, catching me a sharp blow on the back of my hand.

"Get ... away from me. ...Nurse ... get this ... man away from me."

I backed off hurriedly.

From then on, he would not let me near him, threatening me daily with his brass bell every time I went close. I could only observe him from afar and issue orders and prescribe medicine. He continued to deteriorate. His lips developed a bluish tinge and he was plainly exhausted, but he seemed to find new strength whenever I entered the ward and he was ready to ward me off. By the third day of

treating him from a distance it was apparent that he was going to die if he was not put on a ventilator. I told him that.

"Then I ... will ... die. ... I'm ... not ... going on the machine."

I could not just let him die. Yet he would not give consent for intervention. What was I to do? I contacted my medical malpractice insurance. Within an hour they came back to me.

"We have consulted our lawyers. They think that if you put him on a ventilator without his consent the worst that could happen is that he could sue you for assault. We would be prepared to defend you in that event."

Relieved, I developed a strategy. I could not get near him, so I would have to enlist the help of a colleague. Richard was the hospital anaesthetist working for the state. A flamboyant character with a sense of adventure and a taste for the bizarre, he would be the ideal person. I explained my plan.

That afternoon all was ready. The nursing staff had arranged extra oxygen and suction apparatus at the head of the bed and a ventilator was standing by. I hid behind the curtain just next to his bed armed with a tracheal tube to put in his throat and a laryngoscope (an instrument for inserting the tube). Richard sauntered up to Ronnie, a syringe hidden in his hand.

"Hello Ronnie."

"Who ... are you?" asked an exhausted Ronnie suspiciously.

"I'm Richard and I have come to see how you are." He continued talking, distracting him and surreptitiously injected an anaesthetic into the drip in Ronnie's hand.

"What are you ...?" the question trailed off unfinished as Ronnie sank into a coma. Immediately I jumped out from behind the curtain, the nurse rushed up with the oxygen and suction and I slid the tube down his throat. He was connected to the ventilator in less than five minutes. It was progress all the way after that and after five days Ronnie was ready to be weaned and removed from the ventilator. When we could finally take the tube out of his throat and he could speak, I waited with trepidation to see if he would berate me and threaten to sue me. Instead he was effusive in his thanks.

"Dr Walker. Thank you so much for saving my life. I owe it to you. You have no idea how grateful I am!" He became one of my biggest fans and could not stop talking about how I had saved his life. I was just relieved that there were not going to be any court proceedings as I chuckled for weeks about a scene that could have come out of a medical farce.

I was enjoying success as the new anaesthetist in town, but it was coming at a price. As I became busier and busier my wife and children saw less and less of me. Subconsciously it was going to my head. I was the centre of my world.

Amazingly, although I seldom thought of God except as a far-off spectator, when a patient was extremely ill, I would encourage their relatives to pray. I do not think that I really thought that God would hear. I just thought that it was a comforting thing for them to do.

I was lonely spiritually. Sometimes, driving to work there would be the ghost of a prayer at the back of my mind; *"God, where are You?"* but I was hardly conscious of it and I never expected an answer.

However, God was preparing a surprise for me!

Chapter Seven

REVELATION

Call to me and I will answer and show you great and unsearchable things you do not know." (Jer. 33:3)

"Dave, we need you right away. We have someone critically injured who needs surgery now."

I put down the phone, shook my sleepy head and glanced at the clock. It was 1.00 am. A few minutes to dress and I headed for the operating suite. Fifteen minutes later I was in the changing room, all sense of sleep gone and focused on the task ahead, wondering what was in store.

As I hastily pulled on my theatre clothes and boots, grabbing a mask and cap on the way through, I felt the usual surge of excitement. I loved my job. I had now been in anaesthetic practice in Pietermaritzburg for three years and had developed a reputation for handling major cases and following them through to the Intensive Care Unit. To be honest I must admit that my success had filled me with some pride and not a little arrogance. My world revolved around me, my reputation and what I could do for my patients and for society in Pietermaritzburg. As I rushed into the operating room, I had no idea that God had decided it was time to change that.

The patient was already on the operating table. I assessed him quickly.

He was a slightly-built man in his 30s. His clothes had been removed. He lay under a blanket, hardly conscious, cold, clammy, and moaning quietly with every laboured breath. His pulse was barely palpable, and his heart was racing. I smelt alcohol on his breath. The awkward angle of his leg told me that his hip was fractured. His skin and lips were white, drained of all blood and his bulging abdomen told why: he was bleeding internally. I could see that he was close to death. We had to move fast.

I inserted two large cannulae (plastic tubes) into his veins for fluids and blood and then, after the anaesthetic, passed a tube down his throat to control his breathing. After that I thrust a long cannula into his internal jugular vein and threaded it from there down to the upper chamber of his heart. The pressure measurements from this would enable me to assess how much blood he would require.

"OK to start, Robbie."

The scalpel sliced through skin taut and shiny over a distended abdomen. A few deft strokes, and the knife was through into the abdominal cavity. Blood and fluid gushed out, spilling over the drapes and snaking across the floor. The patient's blood pressure plummeted.

"Trouble, Robbie! His blood pressure is way down. I cannot keep up with this blood loss. Could you pack the area and let me catch up?"

Robbie and I worked well together out of mutual respect and a genuine friendship. Balanced and confident in his approach to life as well as his profession, he was an excellent surgeon, working dexterously, unhurriedly, and purposefully. With the patient stabilised, Robbie assessed the damage.

"A ruptured spleen, a torn liver, and probably a tear in his vena cava."

I gave a mental gasp and thought, *"All that and a fractured hip. God help him – (if only He were that kind of God)."* Even if the patient survived the operation, the postoperative course was fraught with danger.

The next hours were filled with focused, intense activity. The patient's spleen was removed and the torn liver packed with haemostatic sponge. That stemmed some of the blood loss, but the torn vena cava was problematic. Blood welled up from the tear every time Robbie removed the pressure swab to suture it. I was pouring stored blood into the patient's veins under pressure as fast as possible to keep up with the blood loss, but this was creating its own problems. Stored blood does not have the clotting factors of our own fresh blood and as he lost litres of his own blood and had it replaced, so he was losing the ability to clot. The bleeding was getting worse. I was giving platelets and plasma to combat this, but the blood bank was running out of stock. The theatre floor on Robbie's side was awash with blood.

Many a patient has died on the operating table from a torn vena cava. It is the largest vein in the body, carrying all the blood from the lower body back to the heart. It is extremely difficult to suture and is always accompanied by huge blood loss, which can be overwhelming. However, with great skill, and patience born of considerable experience, Robbie slowly brought things under control and we knew the patient would survive the operation.

My spirits were soaring. To be part of such a skilled team and to win through was exhilarating. It was 8.00 am. We had been operating for over six hours, but I had not noticed the time, so intense was the concentration and the activity.

The operation was over, but I knew my work was not. It had only changed course. I would now be busy with the patient in the Intensive Care Unit for at least eight hours. His fluid status would be changing by the hour, requiring continual correction. We would have to assist his breathing with a ventilator. His sedation would need to be adjusted; an orthopaedic surgeon consulted about his shattered hip; his blood pressure stabilised; his blood chemistry adjusted, and complications dealt with as they arose.

For three weeks he hovered between death and life as we fought for his survival. He became jaundiced and developed septicaemia (a blood infection). His lungs stiffened from all the blood he had been given and from the shock of so much blood loss. His kidneys failed temporarily from the shock and trauma. Every day was a fight. It was tiring work and it meant hectic days and sleepless nights, but I loved it. It was worth it if we could save his life. During that time, I learnt more about my patient and the circumstances of the accident.

Pete was married and had two young children. He had a regular clerical job. He played cricket at a local club, and liked to stay on after the game drinking with the boys. Things had not gone well on the night of his accident. He had been drinking too much and he and his wife had had a violent argument. He stormed out of the house in a rage, started the car and raced down the driveway. Within minutes he was on the freeway driving furiously, weaving dangerously as his mind, already addled with alcohol, burned with the aftermath of their argument. Inevitably he lost control and the car hurtled off the freeway and into a bridge support. He was not wearing a seat belt.

"Tragic," I thought, *"and so unnecessary. Less of a wild lifestyle and a little more kindness and consideration and this would have been avoided. However, if he survives, surely he will understand how lucky he has been, and he will be a better man for it."*

Finally, after three weeks we could relax a little. It looked as though Pete would live. It was a major medical victory. With a slim chance of surviving all that he had been through, he had beaten the odds.

I was proud of my contribution to Pete's survival. He was discharged from the ICU, but it would take a hip operation and months of slow, painful rehabilitation before he was fit enough for discharge from hospital. I visited him from time to time in the ward. He had little recollection of the incident and his ICU stay.

It was about six months after his final discharge from hospital when I heard news of him again. A colleague mentioned that he had met Pete's wife at a function. I was alert and curious. How had his close encounter with death affected him?

"How is he doing?" I was anticipating good news.

"Well, physically fine. He walks with a bit of a limp, but he's putting on weight and feeling strong."

"And mentally? Emotionally?"

"Nothing has changed. In fact, it is much worse. He is drinking more than he was and he has left his wife and children."

I felt shocked, as if I had been betrayed. After all that effort nothing in his life had changed. What effect had I had — what permanent, life-changing effect? What was my real purpose in life? Was I put on this earth just to save physical lives and make no permanent change to the quality of the whole person? I felt lonely and strangely disconnected from my fellows, my work, and my ambition. Nothing made sense anymore.

So began my search for a God who is involved — not, as I thought some far-off being or force who disinterestedly looks on while we try to do the best we can with our ever-changing circumstances. I recognised that without Someone who could touch hearts and change lives from the inside, what I was doing was superficial and transitory. We are all destined to die. If I prolonged that process by a few years and the person died unchanged on the inside where was the lasting victory?

The Bible says that if we seek God, we will find Him if we seek Him with all our heart. (Jer. 29:13) It took me six months of searching but, true to His word, I found Him. It would be more correct to say that He came to me.

I stayed behind after a particularly moving church service and shared my disappointment in a God who seemed so distant. A couple prayed with me and suggested that I pray and read my Bible.

"Maybe you are not allowing Him to intervene and guide your life." they said. *"You seem very self-sufficient and confident of your own ability. Why don't you try asking for His help even if you think you can do it yourself?"*

Then, after praying as best I knew how, reading a Bible that didn't seem to make much sense, asking Him to help me with the anaesthetics that I thought I had been managing well on my own anyway, and quietly, but desperately asking Him to show me if He was there, and cared, He came.

I awoke very early one morning bathed in the love of Jesus and with His presence filling the room with a kind of all-pervading peace. I knew without a doubt that He is personal and present with us, interested in what we are doing and waiting for us to include Him, through prayer, in all that we do. I spent from 4.00 am till morning in prayer, talking to this wonderful God who, I now realised, had been with me all my life, enabling me and guiding me but whom I had ignored in my egotistical chase for my own glory.

Reluctantly, I left my time of prayer and went to work. Once there I could not help sharing my experience. I was met with enthusiasm from some, but with guarded looks and a polite scepticism from others. That did not dampen my zeal, however. I knew that what I had experienced was real and I started to share the love of God with my patients, encouraging them to trust God with their lives as they prepared for surgery.

In the Intensive Care Unit, particularly, I started to pray with my critically ill patients and their relatives. Before this experience I used to tell the relatives that as intensivists we cannot heal. All we can do is to manipulate the patient's organ functions — heart, blood pressure, breathing, liver and kidneys using drugs, fluids or devices such as a ventilator or kidney machine, keeping them as normal as possible. From then on it is up to the patient. He has to heal himself. Now, with my new-found faith, I would say, more correctly, that from then it is up to God, who looks for our prayers to respond to, and I would offer to pray with them and with my patient.

What an exciting turn my life took as I turned my attention away from myself and what I could do, towards a loving, powerful God and what He can do! I saw His faithfulness in responding to the prayers and the faith of the people that He loved and died for. Overnight I was seeing lives transformed, not just with physical healing – in fact sometimes without physical healing – but with an encounter with the living

God of wholeness, not only health. I hope to introduce you to some of those lives in the rest of the pages of this book.

This book is a testimony to the faithfulness of a God whose ways are not always our ways, but whose conduct is always that of a loving, kind and intensely personal God; a God who loves to intervene when we relate to Him personally in prayer and obedience to His Word.

As you read, you may think, as I did, that God could have acted differently in certain situations. I have learned, however, that we never see the big picture. Our encounter with other people gives us a tiny window into a small moment in their lives. God knows what they have been through, what is yet to come and what thread in the tapestry of their lives is appropriate for that time. The common denominator is that each patient had an encounter with the living God. That encounter made a difference in some way. For some it set them thinking; for others it brought strength; others received physical healing and for others it was a welcome home. All, however, are testimony to a God who is not distant, but who cares and responds to the prayers of His people.

Chapter Eight

A POISONED CHILD

"Jesus said, 'Let the little children to come to me, and do not hinder them; for the kingdom of heaven belongs to such as these.'" (Matt. 19:14)

I looked down on little three-year-old Tessa as she lay semi-conscious, struggling to breathe.

There is something doubly-distressing about a critically ill child. Adults in a life-threatening state arouse a sense of urgency and compassion, but on seeing a desperately ill child something rises up wanting to protect; to shield an innocent life from the harsh realities of a fallen world. Such were my feelings as I examined Tessa. Her ribcage rocked in and out from weakened muscles with each breath, which gurgled through secretions accumulating in her breathing passages. Beside her bed her distraught mother stared unseeing at the monitors, feeling the helplessness of watching while everything was out of her control and in the hands of the attending doctors.

Tessa and John, her older brother by one year, had been playing in the garage at home. They were having a tea party for their toys. They had set out the tea set and teddy and the dolls were sitting around drinking invisible tea from the teacups. The children were joining in drinking from their cups, but it was not realistic enough for little John. They needed some real tea to drink. He found some liquid in the garage, poured it into his sister's cup and gave it to her to drink. It was deadly insecticide!

As the poison swept through Tessa's body it targeted the heart, slowing it down and threatening to stop it in a cardiac arrest. It latched onto her muscles which started twitching and then became progressively weaker. Slowly Tessa was becoming paralysed, impairing her ability to breathe. The toxic molecules attached themselves to her salivary glands making them pour out saliva that threatened to suffocate her.

I debated whether to put her on a ventilator — not a step to be taken lightly with a little child. The tube that one places in the child's trachea has such a small diameter that it can easily block with secretions, cutting off the air supply altogether. I needed to know that it was absolutely necessary before taking this step.

I considered that, although Tessa was in trouble, she was just managing on the maximum dose of antidote that the paediatrician had given her. I had an appendicectomy scheduled for an hour's time. I would reassess her after that. If necessary, we could ventilate her then. A thought nudged forward from the back of my mind that I should pray with her, but I pushed it back. The doctors and nurses were so busy with her and, besides, if I left now, I would have time to get home and have lunch before coming back for the appendicectomy.

As I got into my car the sense that I should have prayed for her grew stronger. Still I ignored it, but all the way home, my mind was filled with one thought, *"I should have prayed with her. I should pray with her. ... "*

I pulled into the driveway of my home, but I could bear it no longer. I turned around and drove straight back to the hospital. I have noticed that sometimes when we disobey God and then repent and do what He is prompting, it is even harder the second time. It is as though He is testing our resolve. Such was the case as I returned. Conditions were not conducive to earnest prayer for Tessa as I entered the ICU. The distressed mother and her sister were there, talking animatedly. Tessa was, if anything, a little worse and the nurse was busy attending to her. I had to interrupt them all.

"Excuse me," I interjected into the mother's conversation, *"I am a committed Christian and I would like to say a prayer for Tessa and ask God to heal her."*

I was unprepared for the reaction. The mother started crying hysterically and began stroking her child. The aunt was trying to comfort the mother and adding to the noise as I laid my hand on the child and tried to pray. I did not feel very spiritual at all. It was an effort to concentrate. All I could do was to lay my hand on Tessa and stammer out some jumbled words above the surrounding chaos, *"Dear God, I ask ... er ... I ask You ... uuh ... I know You love children. Please ... er ... (I cannot think) please heal Tessa in Jesus' Name."*

With that I hastily left to anaesthetise my patient for his appendicectomy. All the way through the appendix operation my mind was on Tessa.

"What a disastrous time." I thought. *"I didn't have a chance to pray properly. I felt nothing. I didn't have a chance to get into any deep prayer."* But I did feel better for having been obedient and having at least attempted to pray.

With the appendicectomy finally over and the patient awake and settled in the recovery room, I hastened through to the ICU. I was met at the door by two very excited nurses.

"Come and see!" they said, jumping up and down as they ushered me into the room.

As I entered, I saw Tessa sitting on her mother's lap, wide awake and drinking milk from a bottle. Ten minutes after I had prayed, Tessa had opened her eyes, sat up and said she was thirsty. All her muscle weakness had gone the secretions that were making her gurgle as she breathed dried up and her head cleared. She was completely healed in an instant.

Three years later I was sitting in church when I felt a tap on my shoulder. It was Tessa's aunt. She was now a Christian and had come to visit our church from up-country. In a church of 500 people she had chosen the seat just behind where I was to sit. She told me that Tessa had been completely healed from that moment in ICU, with no after- effects whatsoever. All the milestones which mark a child's progress were normal and she was a lovely happy child.

I learned several lessons from God's miraculous intervention that day.

Firstly, I learned that even a whisper at the back of our mind can be a prompting from God to allow Him to do a mighty work. He does not whisper for the little things and shout for the big ones. He speaks to us the way He wants to speak to us, and we need to be sensitive and ready to be obedient to the slightest hint that this might be God. That day it was inconvenient with all the people attending her.

In addition, I was hungry, and, because I wanted my lunch, I nearly missed a powerful miracle that showed God's love and power to a family on the brink of tragedy.

Secondly, God is not impressed with form. What He is looking for is obedience. So often I have felt really eloquent in my prayers and thought, *"That was powerful. Surely God will respond to that prayer!"* and little has happened. At other times I have experienced no 'anointing' and yet God has moved powerfully. This certainly was the case with Tessa.

"As the heavens are higher than the earth, so are my ways higher than your ways and my thoughts than your thoughts."
Isa. 55:9

Chapter Nine

AN UNEXPECTED OUTCOME

"Even though I walk through the valley of the shadow of death I will fear no evil, for you are with me." (Ps. 23:4)

"Dr Walker, could I see you privately for a minute?" The request came from one of the ICU sisters after I had completed my ward round.

Her father had been diagnosed with an expanding aortic aneurysm.

The aorta is the main artery in our body, and it carries all the blood from the main pumping chamber of the heart to the lower part of the body. Sometimes a segment of the wall of the artery becomes weak and starts to bulge, much like the bulge in a weakened part of a bicycle tube when it is over-inflated. As it expands, the wall weakens further and eventually bursts, causing catastrophic internal bleeding, which is often fatal. Nowadays it is usually possible to treat the aneurysm with a fairly minor procedure, placing an internal stent within the aorta to strengthen the wall. At the time the sister spoke to me, however, the only solution was a major operation in which the weakened part of the aorta was replaced with a synthetic, flexible tubular graft. It is a major operation requiring management in ICU afterwards. She wanted to know if I would give the anaesthetic to her father for the operation. I went to visit him.

John was a fit man in his early 70s. Like his daughter, he was a committed Christian and, after examining him clinically we had a time just talking about our faith and sharing our mutual love for God. It was always special to find a patient entering a time of crisis trusting in the *Prince of Peace,* our *Comforter* and our *Strength.* We prayed, committing everything that was due to happen the next day to Jesus and I left with a spring in my step. I had so often seen the faithfulness of God when we put ourselves in His hands.

The next day, under the glare of the theatre lights, the scalpel glided cleanly from the top of the abdomen all the way down to the pubis, parting the skin and exposing fat and muscle beneath. Little arteries spurted blood which was deftly dabbed with a swab by the surgical assistant before each offending artery was cauterised closed by the surgeon. Music played softly in the background overridden in part by the bleep ... bleep ... bleep ... of my monitors, the sigh of the ventilator breathing for the patient and the drone of the diathermy machine every time it cauterised an artery. John's operation was under way and it progressed well as I had experienced so often when everything had been committed to God beforehand.

"Access to the aorta is very easy."

Then, *"I'm sewing in the graft. It is fitting perfectly."*

A little while later, *"Opening the clamp. There is very little blood loss."*

John was settled in the ICU afterwards and after just a day there, was ready to be discharged to the ward. Ten days later I arrived as usual to set up for my routine list of operations but was told that they were rushing an emergency patient into my operating theatre. To my dismay it was John. He had suffered a wound disruption.

At the end of an operation all the tissues through which the surgeon sliced to gain access to the operation site are sewn together again. In a way that is no less marvellous for our having grown accustomed to it, the edges fuse together as cells migrate across from each side, eventually forming a scar.

Sometimes, though, this does not happen. Occasionally, due to excessive straining or coughing, some stitches break before the body has time to heal, or the healing process may be delayed through malnutrition or prolonged illness. Then the wound can break open in what is termed a wound disruption. The incision for John's operation ran the whole length of his abdomen. As that long wound ruptured, all his intestines burst out — spewing into the bed!

The body suffers tremendous damage from such a wound disruption. As the bowels hang out of the wound, shock waves race up the nerves to the heart causing it to slow and the blood pressure to drop. Meanwhile the blood supply to the intestines, being stretched tight, fails, the bowels are tinged blue and toxins and bacteria accumulate like an arsenal ready to be discharged to the rest of the body as the bowels are replaced and the blood supply is restored.

When John arrived in the operating room, he was grey, sweating and shocked. He managed a weak smile when he saw me. Rapidly placing an oxygen mask over his face, I proceeded with the anaesthetic as quickly as possible.

It is a relatively simple procedure to place the bowel back in the abdomen and sew the wound closed, but in this case the disruption had taken its toll. John was extremely ill. In the coming days he became worse. The toxins and bacteria in his blood affected his heart; his wound became septic and it appeared that the sepsis had spread to his arterial graft. He lay, grey and gaunt in the ICU, grimacing occasionally in pain as his temperature swung wildly throughout the day.

Each day I was crying out to God. It was a mystery and a great disappointment. We had trusted Him and, after a seemingly good start, it had all gone wrong. Where was God? He was usually so faithful. As I went into ICU for my ward round each morning, I would hope to see signs of improvement. Instead I saw John looking haggard and strained, often sweating and in pain. Medically, too, the surgeon and I could think of nothing more that we could do. We had reviewed John's case time and again and changed his medication, to no effect. His kidneys and heart were now starting to fail as he developed a blood infection.

John and I prayed together but I could see it was a struggle for him and an act of the will to praise God under those circumstances. Usually I prayed and trusted that John, his face sometimes contorted with pain, was concurring. With no external evidence, we had to believe that God had heard our prayers before his operation and that He was still in control. More than that, we had to believe that all things work together for good for those who love Him and are called according to His purpose. Doubts assailed me with every declaration of these truths as we prayed, but I had to put the doubts aside and trust that God is who He says He is; not only loving and faithful but infinitely wiser than we are.

After five days, as I was walking to the ICU, I braced myself to face, yet again, a man I regarded as a friend, who was consumed with fighting pain and fever and a failing heart. To my surprise I was met with a broad, genuine smile and a glow on his face that you could see from the door.

"What happened?" I asked with curiosity and a stirring excitement.

"I met Jesus!"

"You did WHAT?!"

"Yes, I met Jesus last night. As I was drifting off to sleep, He came and stood at the end of my bed. His power and His love just enveloped me. It was glorious."

He still struggled to speak in his weak state, but there was no doubting his enthusiasm as he continued.

"Then He took me by the hand and together we visited all of my favourite places in Pietermaritzburg. We went home, we went to my favourite restaurant, and then we went to World's View, where we could overlook the city. Finally, He brought me back here and as He left, He said, 'Now don't forget to praise me.' "

I said, *"Well, let's do just that."* I held his hand and we started to pray. Eloquent praise poured from his lips in easy, fervent worship. It was supernatural empowerment. He could not have done that the night before. Whether in a vision or a dream, I did not doubt that John had experienced Jesus personally in a way that had profoundly affected him.

It would be wonderful to say that John was physically healed, but he was not. We struggled medically, doing everything we could to save him, but he continued to deteriorate and finally closed his eyes to this world. However, through his suffering, while he was still conscious, there was restfulness in his spirit. God, in His mercy, had given John a glimpse of home — true home in the presence of Jesus and, though marked with suffering, given him assurance that he would soon be there.

I was deeply disappointed in the outcome of John's operation and I mourned for him. I did not like to see him in pain the way that he was, and I so wanted him to get well. Yet, when we cried out to Him, Jesus came. There is a deep mystery in suffering. Nowhere does God say that He will protect us from it. What He does promise, however, is that He will walk with us through it. Many people, having experienced great suffering through bereavement, persecution, financial hardship or illness testify that those were the times when they felt closest to God.

Jesus, more literally than usual, walked with John through His suffering. In the spirit, He took him by the hand and allowed him to relive his favourite places and to say goodbye to them.

If you are enduring hardship or pain, God is not far away. Sometimes the best experience is not relief, but the all-pervading power and love of His manifest presence. And He is faithful. If we pray, He will come.

"You will seek me and find me when you seek me with all your heart." Jer. 29:13

Chapter 10

The COMPASSIONATE HEART of JESUS

"And I will ask the Father, and he will give you another Counsellor to be with you forever."
(John 14:16)

Sometimes the most innocuous, well-intentioned actions have dire consequences that leave us with regrets forever. In vain we relive the scene, wishing somehow that we could reverse our actions — start again with a better knowledge.

Six-year-old Jason had been ill with influenza and was tucked up in bed. Flushed in his face, with a runny nose, a cough, and a high fever, he was miserable. He was given medicine which contained aspirin, and his parents prepared to nurse him for a few days until he recovered. But Jason did not get better. In fact, he started vomiting and became a little confused. He was admitted to hospital. Two days later Jason was still vomiting, and was very drowsy, crying out sporadically and thrashing around in the bed as if hallucinating. The paediatrician now had no doubt of the diagnosis. He turned to the parents, his face grave. …

"I am afraid your child has Reye's Syndrome."

Very, very rarely when a child is given aspirin, it has terrible consequences. For reasons yet unknown, the little person develops an inflammation of the brain and liver. It is extremely uncommon and can sometimes be quite mild, but in over a third of cases it is fatal. Reye's Syndrome, as this illness is called, is more likely to happen if the aspirin is given while the child has a viral illness such as influenza or chicken pox. Today no children's medicines contain aspirin and there are notices on aspirin products warning against their use in children.

Jason was brought to the Intensive Care Unit where he was drip-fed to keep him well hydrated and where any abnormalities in his blood chemistry were corrected. There is no cure for Reye's Syndrome. One can only rectify any correctable abnormalities and wait for the body to recover.

The child slipped deeper and deeper into a coma. Looking down at his little form in the ICU one could not guess how close to death he was. He seemed a normal, chubby, freckle-faced little six-year-old with curly, red-brown locks, who was enjoying a good, deep, restful sleep. Yet if one could have looked internally one would have seen a brain that was inflamed and swelling, becoming tighter and tighter inside the skull, till soon the pressure would be so high that no blood could surge through the arteries to supply vital oxygen and nutrients. One would see a liver engorged and yellow, its cells accumulating fat as they struggled vainly to break it down.

Jason's parents kept a constant vigil by his bed. Visiting hour rules were waived for this couple whose world was falling apart as they watched their sleeping child who would probably never awaken. I was not involved clinically with Jason's case, but I walked past his bed at least twice a day to go to see my patients. Like many others I felt an ache for the parents, but I could not see how I could become involved. Medically I had nothing to contribute and I did not want to intrude into the parents' private grief. Nevertheless, it tugged at my heart each time I walked past them.

After a few days it became apparent that, short of a miracle, Jason would die. His breathing was getting deeper, more like a regular sighing and his pulse was irregular.

I had been praying for Jason as I worked on the adjacent patient near his little unconscious body. I had also been reading a book called In His Steps, by Charles Sheldon. It is a Christian novel about a community in a small town who decided that, for a year, every major decision they made would be guided by what Jesus would do in that situation. As I was standing by my patient but watching Jason's distraught dad beside his sighing child, I was having a conversation with God. The book came to mind and I thought, "What would You do right now, Jesus?"

What would Jesus have done? Into my mind came stories from the Bible of how, without her invitation, He walked across to a grieving widow in the town of Cain and raised her son from the dead; of how He approached a man who was waiting unsuccessfully by a pool to be healed and healed him. Without waiting for them to come to Him, he moved, out of compassion, into their lives. And I remembered how He said, *"Let the little children come to Me."* Surely if He were here, He would approach this suffering dad and touch his son.

"Lord Jesus" I prayed under my breath, *"I know that if you were here you would walk across, touch that child and heal him. All I can do is to walk across in your place."*

I moved towards the dad who looked at me with eyes red and swollen from weeping. *"You don't know me,"* I began, *"but I am a doctor here. I am also a committed Christian. I know about your little boy and I would love to pray for him if you would let me."*

He nodded, too afraid to speak. As I prayed, I felt the sting of tears on my own cheeks. I longed for Jesus to heal that little boy. How wonderful it would be to see his little freckled face laughing and alive. I prayed for the dad beside me and for Jason's mother, for strength and the comforting presence of Jesus.

No dramatic healing occurred. Jason died soon afterwards.

A year later I was taking an evening stroll when, to my surprise I saw Jason's dad coming towards me. The family had moved into a house in my street. We greeted one another warmly, though I had only met him formally on that afternoon in ICU. He kept thanking me profusely for my prayers for Jason.

"You have no idea what that did for us," he said, *"to have him lifted up to Jesus as he was dying. It was like putting him into His arms."*

I suspect that there was even more to it than that, wonderful though that was.

Whenever there is the death of someone dear, guilt feelings arise, often quite irrationally. The wife of the husband who has a heart attack may feel guilty for not having looked after his diet better, even if she had done her best in that regard. The husband of a wife dying of cancer may, without reason, blame himself, thinking that they might have picked it up earlier had he been more alert or caring. When your child has been treated with a medicine that he reacts badly to, it is so easy, although wrongly, to blame yourself. But God knows the truth. The reason for having given the medicine was a caring one, and God sees the heart. So, to parents, heartbroken and perhaps too guilt-ridden to approach Him, He sent me. He took the initiative as He had with the widow of Cain and with the man at the pool of Bethsaida and approached them through me. Though He did not heal their boy, He allowed the father to be a part of lifting him up into His arms; and He touched their lives and showed them that He had not forsaken them and was there for them to draw near to Him for comfort and strength.

How quick we sometimes are to judge ourselves and to think that God does the same. Yet He is a Friend and a Healer. A true friend likes us even when we do not like ourselves and He is as true a friend as we can ever find. And His healing does not always come by making the situation go away, but by walking through it with us as an understanding, loving companion. He is well qualified for the role.

After all, He has already been there:

"My soul is overwhelmed with sorrow to the point of death." –
Jesus (Mark 14:34)

"A man of sorrows and familiar with suffering."
Isaiah, describing Jesus (Isa. 53:3)

"The Lord is close to the broken-hearted and rescues those who are crushed in spirit." (Ps. 34:18)

"Blessed are those who mourn, for they will be comforted." (Matt. 5:4)

.

Chapter Eleven

PARTNERING with GOD

"They will place their hands on sick people, and they will get well." (Mark 16:18)

Fourteen-year-old Pierre had enjoyed a wonderful holiday with his family in a game reserve. They all arrived home just in time for the start of the next term. Pierre was looking forward to telling his friends at school all about it. While at school, however, he did not feel well and he went to sick bay. There the school nurse was alarmed to find that his temperature was soaring. Within minutes he was shaking uncontrollably and complaining of feeling cold. Then he became delirious. He was rushed to hospital. His breathing was now rapid, and his lips had a bluish tinge. That evening he required assistance from a ventilator to help his breathing. Pierre had contracted malaria while in the game reserve.

When a malarial mosquito infects a person, the parasites enter the blood cells. In severe cases the cells clump together and, instead of carrying life-giving oxygen to the body, they stop the blood from reaching the tissues and deprive them of oxygen. This is what had happened to Pierre. The disease had affected his lungs and, quite probably his brain, in what is known as cerebral malaria. He deteriorated rapidly and I took over the management of his case after two days.

I looked down upon a young athletic boy with short-cropped, sandy hair. His handsome face was now invaded with tubes in his mouth and through his nose. His lips, enclosing the tube and distorted with strapping, were tinged with blue and his cheeks, too, had a bluish flush. He was under sedation, so that he did not appear to be in any distress, but the equipment surrounding him told the true story. The ECG monitor showed a heart that was racing; the machine measuring his blood oxygen confirmed what could be seen at a glance from his lips and cheeks. He was desperately starved of oxygen. Most striking, however, was the ventilator, straining under dangerous pressures to push alarmingly small volumes of oxygen into lungs solid with fluid and collapsed air sacs. I was at a loss at what else to do. I prayed and pushed the ventilator settings a little higher. Then I started phoning the experts around the country. They were all pessimistic. They advised that I was already pushing the limits for the ventilator settings beyond the safe parameters, but could give no advice on how I could alter that. (Today we have much more sophisticated ventilators that give us more options, but they were not available for Pierre). The gloomy prognosis from all the experts was that Pierre would probably die from the complications of his disease, but if he survived, we would never be able to wean him from the ventilator.

I had been laying hands on him and praying but to no visible effect. Each day I faced the family in the ICU waiting room and each day the conversation was the same.

"How is he, Doc? Any improvement?"
I would look into the worried faces of his mom, dad, and sister – faces drawn and strained from sleepless nights.

"I'm sorry, he is just the same. I am doing all I can. He is in God's hands. We need to pray."

And we would join hands and bow our heads and call out to God. One day, after the same conversation, I suggested that we should all go into the ICU and lay hands on him. There, with our hands resting on Pierre's barely moving chest and with the sound of the ventilator straining in the background in short, rapid hisses, we called on the God of compassion and architect of the family unit to preserve this family and to have mercy on the young man. Almost imperceptibly, I thought I heard the ventilator tone change. A little more oxygen was entering his lungs. I did a test. It was true. His level of oxygen, though still critical, had improved very slightly.

For the next week, every day, the family and I gathered around the young boy's bed to lay hands on him and pray, and slowly his blood oxygen level improved. After a week it was at a level that would at least provide enough oxygen to the organs for them to function. Caring for him was hard, emotionally-taxing work and the improvement was very gradual. Every week would bring another minor victory and another cause for worry. Would the ventilator pressures precipitate a crisis? Had the malaria and the lack of oxygen for such a long time affected his brain? Would he have permanent brain damage? Would he get a chest infection? There was so much that could go wrong. With such a critical case being in ICU for so long it is unusual for there not to be many complications along the way.

I was still in occasional contact with the experts around the country. They remained pessimistic. We would be unable to wean him from the ventilator. And even if we did manage to do so, they said that he would be a respiratory cripple for the rest of his life.

"Your young patient will be unable to walk without stopping for breath," they said. *"He will always be desperate for air."*

We continued to pray. Believing nurses laid hands on him. His family, when they visited, prayed. As long as we called on God, he improved. We were able to slowly reduce the pressures, then the oxygen. Then there was celebration as Pierre was removed from the ventilator and could breathe on his own. As we reduced the sedation, we waited anxiously to see his mental function. He opened his eyes and looked around. We called his name. He responded. We asked him questions. He understood them. Within a day he was alert and oriented. Though frail and weak, he proved to be an intelligent young boy with a delightful sense of humour.

After three months, Pierre was discharged from the Intensive Care Unit. He was off the ventilator, breathless, but breathing by himself. He was discharged from hospital two months later. I was anxious to know if the predictions of the experts would be correct. Would breathlessness be a constant haunting companion? His father contacted me after six months. Pierre had run a cross country race and had just played in a tennis tournament. His breathing was normal.

What we saw was a miracle, but it was not instantaneous, and it was not without employing all the knowledge, expertise, dedication and care that we had available. Nevertheless, no doctor could account for the complete recovery of a brain assailed by malaria and seriously deprived of oxygen for more than ten days, and lungs that, contrary to the opinions of the best experts in the land, functioned normally. For all the time and effort that it took it was no less miraculous.

Often, we expect God to do it all on His own. Sometimes He does and, of course, He is perfectly able to do that. Most times, however, He chooses to partner with us. The greatest way that He partners with us is in prayer. However, just as, after telling His disciples to pray for workers for the harvest field, Jesus commanded them to go as the workers they had prayed for (Matt. 9:37 – 10:1), so He will use us to be instruments in the very answer to the prayers that we have been praying. It has been my privilege to combine the expertise that He has given me with prayer and to see God do, with medicine, far above all I could ask or imagine or that medicine alone can do. I cannot count the number of times that patients have recovered against huge odds as medicine is combined with prayer.

When we pray, we should also be listening. Might it be that we could be the answer to our prayer?

"And the prayer offered in faith will make the sick person well; the Lord will raise him up." (James 5:15)

Chapter Twelve

REPRIEVE from DEATH in a STUBBORN MAN

"Seek the Lord while he may be found; call on him while he is near." (Isa. 55:6)

"It seems a bit futile, Dave, but we have to try."

The surgeon and I were discussing a patient who had a large tumour in his abdomen.

When I had examined him, he looked like someone in the terminal stages of cancer. Gaunt and weak, panting quietly as he breathed, he stared out from eyes deep in skull-like sockets. In his face and ribs, he was as thin as a victim of the Holocaust. In striking contrast were a large distended belly and hands and feet that were swollen with oedema, so that in his peripheries he looked like a bag of water. As I sat him up in bed, his back was equally swollen with fluid. I let him down gently and examined his abdomen. A large lump could be felt and there was evidence of a lot of fluid. A chest X-ray showed fluid on his lungs.

We were out of earshot as we discussed his options. Pete, the surgeon spoke up.

"I know it seems hopeless, but despite that large tumour I cannot find any evidence of secondary spread. We need to give him a chance." This was in the days before the sophisticated diagnostic imaging aids that we have today.

I was concerned about all the oedematous fluid that he was carrying. As we did the workup tests the reason for the fluid became apparent. He was so malnourished that his blood proteins were extremely low. It is these proteins that hold the water in the capillaries, through osmotic pressure. The operation, in someone so malnourished, would be very hazardous and I was not optimistic that we would be able to do anything for the patient. He looked as if it would be but a few months before he succumbed to the cancer. Nevertheless, I had to agree with the surgeon. We did not have a definite diagnosis and without intervention he would certainly die. So we scheduled him for surgery.

Mike was a guarded, reserved man. I tried to set him at ease before his operation, telling him of God's love and faithfulness if we would entrust ourselves to him. He looked at me with inscrutable eyes gazing from gaunt sockets and mumbled a non-committal answer. I tried to read what was going on behind that impassive face. Was he too ill to respond? Was he nervous, knowing that he was looking death in the eye? Had he had a bitter experience that made it hard for him to trust? Whatever it was, it was difficult for me to reassure him. He acquiesced to my saying a prayer with him before his operation, but it did nothing to alter his guarded resistance to any personal contact.

On the day of operation, I needed time for preparation before the surgeon could operate. I sat Mike on the operating table and, under a local anaesthetic, thrust a large needle into each side of his chest to drain out the fluid.

Having thus allowed his lungs to expand to their full capacity I could anaesthetise him.

Once he was asleep, Pete started the operation. As he sliced across the skin, water trapped in the patient's tissues seeped from the wound and trickled down his abdomen. All the organs in his belly were bloated and waterlogged and needed to be handled with great care.

Considering Mike's condition, the operation went very well. The surgeon removed a portion of his intestine that was filled with a large tumour. There was no sign that it had spread anywhere else and the reason was apparent when the pathologist's report came through while we waited in surgery for the result. This was not a cancer, but an amoeboma. Mike had had an attack of amoebic dysentery earlier in his life and this benign tumour was a rare complication of that. In fact, an amoeboma is not really a true tumour. If we could get him through the recovery period, he should be fine. But getting him through would be difficult. He was so malnourished, with so much fluid in his tissues, that healing would be difficult and infection almost a certainty.

Finally, with the operation complete, he was settled in the ICU.

I have never seen a man so filled with oedematous fluid. When we turned him on his left side, his right, upper side was skin and bone but the lower skin bulged like a bag with all the water. Turn him on his right and all the fluid moved across to the other side. There was also the problem of the fluid in his lungs. I drained them every day; and as I came to do that, I would offer to pray with him. Initially there was that same guarded agreement each time, but as he slowly recovered, so there was a remarkable change. It

61

seemed that he would look forward to my coming and would be waiting for me to say, *"Shall we pray?"*

Mike's personality changed, too. Slowly his guard came down to reveal a fun-loving man with a dry sense of humour and a quirky enjoyment of the slightly bizarre. It was wonderful to see. Yet still, there was that reserve about anything spiritual. He

was sceptical about God's love, but he enjoyed our times of prayer and said, a few times after we had prayed, *"You have definitely got something there, Doc."* I wished it were more than that. I wished he could see that it was not the prayer, but the person of Jesus responding to the prayer. Neither was it me, but it was Jesus in me.

And yet, despite Mike's scepticism, God was healing him. Despite the high risk of developing complications, he improved progressively with no major problems, although he was in the ICU for two weeks.

I told him about responding to all that Jesus was doing for him, but, though he was now enjoying our prayer times, he remained guarded. One day he spoke of a dream he had had the night before. *"I saw Jesus,"* he said, *"and He told me that He would call me to follow Him, but not yet."*

"I doubt that was Jesus, Mike," I replied. *"He clearly says, 'Now is the time for salvation.' When He has made a way for us to come out of condemnation and into God's love why would He want anyone to wait a minute longer than he had to?"*

I had become a friend of this fascinating, funny, yet reserved man. It was a joy to see him put on weight and to witness the soggy limbs and torso lose their fluid and become firm and stronger. What a pleasure it was, finally, to see him get out of bed and take a few tentative steps after looking so close to death. How desperately I wanted him to go further than just enjoying our prayer times, to acknowledge the hand of God in his healing.

Finally, I had to say goodbye to Mike as he was discharged. I never fully got past his reserve in spite of our friendship. As I saw him discharged, my mind went to the Biblical story of the ten lepers. They came to Jesus who healed them all, with instructions to go and show themselves to the priest. Only one came back and Jesus commended him and said a strange thing; *"Your faith has made you well."* (Luke 17:11-19). Were they not all made well? I think our understanding of healing is sometimes too small. The other nine lepers received physical healing, but the one who turned back received wholeness. I have seen this in many of my patients who respond in gratitude to God. Not only do they receive physical healing, but they come into a new realisation of God's love, which changes the way they view their lives and respond. They learn to trust God and to discover His faithfulness and power, which enables them to face future trials with a different outlook and an inner strength.

Yet the choice is always ours. God, like a true gentleman, always gives us the option. He will demonstrate His love, even lavish it on those who are far from Him, with profound physical healing and the repeal of an apparent death sentence, as he did with Mike, but He will never force Himself on us. Come to think of it, how could He? Love always must be voluntary to be true.

I have often wondered what happened to Mike. Perhaps, down the path of his life, a crisis came that caused him to remember his time in the ICU and God's response to prayer. Perhaps that has triggered a move towards trust and commitment. I hope so. I grew to care for him and I know that the God who restored him when he was so close to death is also waiting, with the eagerness of the father of the prodigal, to welcome him into His family. There is so much more than physical healing that God wants to give us, but the choice is always ours.

"For God so loved the world that he gave his one and only Son, that whoever believes in him should not perish but have everlasting life." (John 3:16)

Chapter thirteen

PERSONAL TRIAL

"Trust in the Lord with all your heart and lean not on your own understanding." (Prov. 3:5)

I waited anxiously outside the operating room. The surgeon, a friend and colleague, emerged smiling.

"All looks fine." He shook my hand reassuringly. *"There was nothing suspicious on the frozen section. We will, of course have to wait for the formal sections, but it seems OK."*

We had been in Pietermaritzburg for sixteen years. After seeing God work powerfully during that time, it seemed we were about to face our own personal trial. A few days before, Penny had discovered a small lump in her breast and we had consulted my friend Bernie who recommended that, while it looked innocent, we should have it removed for examination. After the surgeon's optimism it seemed our trial would be a trivial one. The evening after the operation, Penny and I celebrated with grateful hearts.

Three days later I was in the operating theatre when Bernie peered around the door and called me aside. He looked grave. *"The laboratory result has just come back on Penny's lump, Dave. They have found cancer there."*

I was quiet as the news struggled to be real in my mind. *"Does she know?"*

"I have just been round to the house to tell her." "How did she take it?"

"She seemed fine."

She would. Never one for histrionics, she would have thanked him for the news and been friendly and chatty. I could not wait to get home. That evening, with the children asleep, we discussed the way forward with a strange sense of unreality. In a detached way we discussed my wife losing a breast as if we were deciding where to go for our next holiday. Finally, we turned out the light and tried to sleep. At two in the morning I awoke. Penny was already awake. I made us some tea and we lay in the dark for hours, confiding whatever was on our hearts. That time, repeated often in the course of the year, was — like a weeping jewel — exquisitely precious in its intimacy, yet so painful; so close, yet so crowded with unfinished thoughts.

We decided that Penny should have a full mastectomy with no reconstruction, and that we would like it done as soon as possible. So it was that three days later my beautiful wife lost her breast to the surgeon's knife. Chemotherapy started three weeks later. She took her first tablets on a Wednesday morning and we waited for side effects. She was fine all day.

"This won't be so bad," we thought, *"if the tablets do not affect her. We can manage bouts of nausea every three weeks from the intravenous drugs."*

Then, while we were having supper on the Thursday, Penny became quiet and unresponsive. She sat, unmoving, her face impassive, staring ahead through blank eyes. Any question was answered in a muttered monosyllable. She seemed to have moved into a cavernous, dark depression beyond any contact. I helped her to bed. One hour later the vomiting came — gut-wrenching, exhausting, humiliating vomiting only partly relieved by the drugs given to counteract it. For the next three days I lost my darling to an alien, solitary prison. Like someone in a catatonic stupor, she lay in bed staring unseeing at the window, answering questions in dull, expressionless monosyllables, and moving only to reach for the basin to be sick. My weekend was fully absorbed in trying to feed her fluids, holding a basin while she was sick, washing her, settling her, only to rush for the basin yet again. Then, on the Sunday evening, like the lifting of a veil, she miraculously came back to life. She entered our world once more, becoming alert, interactive and her usual bright, positive self. It was wonderful to have her back. The next morning, she was ready to go back to work, with no sign of what she had been through the whole weekend.

This was to become the pattern of our lives for the next ten months. Every Wednesday she took her tablets and every Thursday at supper she slipped out of our world into a dark, morose, retching hell for three days, emerging on Sunday evening alert and ready for the next week. All other activities were put on hold while we wrestled with the consequences of her cancer. The intravenous chemotherapy every three weeks affected her heart and left her debilitated, breathless, and weak.

Yet through it all, God showed His love and care. The engineers who employed Penny were very understanding. She was put on a four-day week with full pay and loved and

67

mollycoddled as though she was their daughter. People that we hardly knew sent messages of encouragement, urging us to continue to look to God. Others brought meals or brought her back from the hospital when I could not manage it, or brightened our house with flowers. For Penny's part, she spoke openly about her cancer and what it was like to have only one breast.

It opened the door for many conversations with women who were curious and afraid, demystifying it and allowing them to express their fears and have those fears allayed.

Finally, the gruelling course ended. It had taken its toll, but Penny was a fighter. She joined an organisation called *"Walk for Life",* and within six months she was fit.

And there was no sign of the cancer. After five years she was pronounced cured.

Through it all, God continued to show Himself in my work situations as I prayed with my patients before their operations and in the ICU. Some were moved to tears as I said a simple prayer with them on the evening before their operation; others experienced a "peace beyond understanding" replacing their fear as they entrusted the coming events to God; and others found a freedom to express emotions previously kept deeply hidden but which emerged in the bond that forms as people pray together.

Occasionally there were miraculous events that stand out today like beacons pointing to a powerful, caring God.

"Praise is to the Lord, to God our Saviour, who daily bears our burdens." (Ps. 68:19)

Chapter Fourteen

DROWNING

"Cardiac arrest in Casualty! Cardiac arrest in Casualty!"
The voice came urgently over the intercom. I was close by
at the pharmacy and ran into the emergency area. Four or
five people   nurses and white-coated interns —were
bustling around a trolley in frantic activity. I took in the scene
as I raced to them.

A four-year-old boy in wet shorts lay grey and limp on the
trolley. Two enthusiastic interns had inserted a tube into his
windpipe and were ventilating him with oxygen, while all
eyes were fixed on a monitor which showed an ECG trace.
There was regular electrical activity, albeit quite abnormal
in its shape.
"Does he have a heartbeat?" I asked quickly, as I felt for a
pulse.
"You can see that he does on the ECG." The intern
looked puzzled by my question.
*"That is not a heartbeat. That is electrical activity, but that
does not push the blood around. Continue with CPR*
(cardiopulmonary resuscitation) *until there is a pulse. How
long was he without an ECG trace?"*

"About five minutes. We shocked him three times. We couldn't get an intravenous line, so we gave him adrenaline down his endotracheal tube." (That was the tube going into his windpipe.) *"We have just got a trace now."*

As the interns continued with CPR, I rapidly inserted a cannula into the child's femoral vein and administered adrenaline. Within a few minutes the little grey body flushed pink and we could feel a pulse. Calling for a torch, I pressed gently on his eyelids to open them and looked at his pupils. They were widely dilated. I could not see them contract to the light. This looked bad. Dilated pupils which do not react to light are a sign of severe brain damage. After ten minutes of a stable blood pressure and with a regular heartbeat the child remained limp and motionless and did not start breathing. After twenty minutes he was still not breathing and his body was stiffening, arms extended and head back in the posture of severe brain damage. My heart was sinking. Then I heard the story of what had happened, which sent a chill to my heart.

Little Andrew was playing in the garden while his parents were in the house. Suddenly the mother noticed that he was missing. His hat was floating in their murky swimming pool. Peering into the cloudy water they could not see him. The father was not concerned.

"He is probably in the street. I'll go and look for him."

He went out by the gate, calling him. The mother, still worried that he could be in the pool, ran into the house, changed into her bathing costume, and walked around in the pool, feeling with her legs. Her leg brushed up against something. She knew it was Andrew, but she could not reach him to get him out. Screaming hysterically, she ran to her husband.

70

Together they used the pool skimming net to fish him out. They dumped his lifeless body on the car's back seat and drove furiously to the hospital. It was a twenty-minute drive. At no time did Andrew receive any CPR.

As I listened with horror to the story, I was surprised that Andrew's heart had started at all during resuscitation, but even so it all seemed futile. With such a long time without oxygen his brain could not survive. My mind was filled with scenes from a case we had had in our ICU six months before. A trained ICU sister was visiting friends who had a portable swimming pool. Suddenly she noticed her child lying face down in the water. Hastily she pulled him out. He was not breathing. She immediately administered CPR and he regained a pulse and started breathing but remained unconscious. He lay in our ICU in a vegetative state, convulsing occasionally, for six months before he finally died. He had had resuscitation almost immediately and yet had not survived. Who knows how long Andrew had been without a heartbeat and not breathing before he received any resuscitation at all!

When implicated in a tragedy involving a child, something rises in the depth of my being like a deep primeval cry of *"No!"* It is not fair for a young life to be stripped of all its potential and just cease to exist. It is not the way it was meant to be. It shakes the order of the universe. I was so taken up with all the activity and the tragedy of seeing that dear little boy unconscious on the Emergency Room trolley, wet, tousled hair staining the sheet beneath with a wet ring; a tube now plastered firmly in place distorting his little mouth that I did not even think to pray.

The paediatrician arrived to take over the case. The boy was wheeled to the paediatric ward to be ventilated there

71

and I stood, feeling alone and sad in the Casualty Ward. The interns were proud of the work that they had done in restoring a heartbeat, but I wondered if they had done the right thing. I could not rid my mind of the spectre of the other little boy lying, convulsing day after day, in the ICU. When I was alone, I did pray, although, I confess, not with much faith. In my mind I lifted the child up into God's presence and I think my prayer was more asking Him not to let him linger on as I had seen the other child do. And I prayed for comfort for the parents.

The following evening, I went on a preoperative visit to the paediatric ward to see a patient for my operating list. My mind was on Andrew but I hesitated to ask, expecting the worst. Finally, I cleared my throat and tried to sound casual.

"You know the little boy that was brought in having drowned? Is he still here?"

"Oh yes," the nurse replied. *"We have taken the tube out of his throat."*

"What! Is it OK to do that?"

"Yes. He opened his eyes and started coughing. The doctor took out the tube and he asked for a cup of tea."

I was astounded. *"I am the doctor who resuscitated him in Casualty. Can I see him?"*

I bounded up to his cot. Then I examined him carefully. He understood me and spoke normally, answering all my questions. His neck seemed a little weak and he appeared to be partially blind. He could see my fingers when I put them in front of his eyes, but he could not count them. The following day, as soon as I could, I visited the ward. By now he was sitting upright in bed playing with his toys. His neck was strong and there was no doubt that he could see. How my heart sang with wonder at our good, good God.

I met the parents and confirmed the story of how he was found in the swimming pool. They said that, although they were 'not strong believers', they had mobilised their friends to pray for Andrew. No doubt their friends had prayed with more faith than I had!

Andrew developed a severe chest infection which had to be vigorously treated, but he was discharged from hospital fit and well. Six months later I met the paediatrician in the corridor of the hospital. He pulled me to one side, excitement in his voice. *"I have just seen Andrew for a check- up. All his milestones are absolutely normal for his age."* He, too, was delighted and acknowledged the miracle. God seems to have endowed children with a special abundance of His grace to receive healing. Not only has He bestowed them with a greater resilience in recovering from an onslaught on their health, but they seem to recover more completely. Andrew's healing, however, was more than that.

Given the train of events, especially the time interval before he was resuscitated, there is no doubt that this was a sovereign, miraculous healing from a God who loves children and had a plan for Andrew's life which He did not want cut short by the enemy.

Jesus expressed indignation when the disciples tried to stop the children being brought to Him. He used them as a model of how we should approach Him. Our first instinct, when a child is sick, should be to present them to their loving Father. Without our acquired scepticism and negative judgements they seem to have a ready access to the throne of Grace.

"From the lips of children and infants you have ordained praise ...'to silence the foe and the avenger." (Ps. 8:2)

Chapter Fifteen

A DIFFICULT MAN and the POWER of BLESSING

"But I tell you: Love your enemies and pray for those who persecute, that you may be sons of your Father in heaven."
Matt. 5:44

"I'm sorry, darling, I have to rush."
I gave Penny a hasty kiss as I headed for the door. Then I heard her comment, *"That is your most common remark these days."* And I knew it was time for a change.

I had been in private practice for thirteen years and the busyness was taking its toll on my family. I was seeing little of my children at a vital time in their lives and Penny and I were passing one another in a hectic lifestyle that left little time for anything but superficialities. There was a vacancy for a full-time post as Head of the Anaesthetic Department at Grey's Hospital and I applied for it and was accepted. That was when I encountered Arthur.

The patient was asleep on the operating table. As his chest rose and fell rhythmically with each breath of the ventilator, the monitors bleeped comfortingly, displaying a stable blood pressure and pulse rate, good oxygenation, and normal carbon dioxide levels. Intravenous fluids dripped slowly into a vein in his arm. He was ready for surgery. The sister had painted the patient's abdomen with iodine and covered him with green sterile towels, leaving an area exposed for the slice of the surgeon's knife.

Now we were waiting for the new Chief Surgeon.

Shortly after I joined the Anaesthetic Department at Grey's Hospital, the Department of Surgery appointed a new Chief. This was to be our introduction to him.

Arthur emerged from the scrub room, pulling on his gloves.

"Hi, I'm Dave," I said, refraining from extending my hand, since he was scrubbed and gowned. With no more than a quick glance in my direction and a grunt as an acknowledgement, he turned to the sister and gave a curt order.

"Knife!"

During the operation there was little conversation and no interaction with me. Thus began a tense, uneasy relationship which did not improve over the following weeks.

Arthur was a short, stocky man with bushy eyebrows shading piercing eyes. He was a person who reacted impulsively to the moment, laughing harshly at what he saw as funny, ready to argue vehemently if he disagreed, and riding roughshod over people's opinions and feelings. While he was an excellent surgeon, he was abrasive, not averse to making derisory remarks at another's expense and apparently oblivious to the pain that he was causing. I was particularly angered when he was rude to the nursing staff in his theatre, reducing them, at times, to tears.

An incident in the ICU precipitated a direct confrontation. Part of my mandate as Anaesthetic Chief was to run the ICU, having full clinical responsibility for the state-funded patients. I started my ward round as usual one day in my customary routine, examining a patient who had been operated on by Arthur a few days before.

"We agreed to start small feeds through his nasogastric tube yesterday. How is that going?"

The sister looked a little embarrassed. *"It has not been done, doctor."*

"Oh! And his intravenous fluids? Have they been altered according to my orders?"

"No, doctor. Dr Arthur changed your orders."

I looked at the chart. Two diagonal lines had been scored across the pages of my orders and new orders were written below. Seething inwardly, I sought him out. He was unrepentant. *"You were wrong. It is too early to start feeding him."*

"Well, at least consult me!"

"Why should I? You were wrong!"

Life became difficult and I found myself tensing whenever I realised I was doing Arthur's operating list. As my anger grew, so did my desire for retribution and I started a game of subtle character assassination. At every turn, though he was a good surgeon, I would find reasons to criticise him, usually out of his earshot. I criticised his interpersonal skills, I criticised his clinical etiquette and even, when I could, his surgical skills. However, as I tried to destroy him, so I was being destroyed. Though I did not notice it at first, I was losing my joy and my prayers were becoming prosaic.

Then one day, during my quiet time with God, I read this from the book of Romans: *"Bless those who persecute you;*

bless and do not curse." (Rom. 12:14) and *"If your enemy is hungry, feed him; if he is thirsty, give him something to drink."* (Rom. 12:20)

I knew God was talking to me about Arthur and my attitude and actions, but I was reluctant to obey. It seemed unreasonable and I could not imagine myself engaging with him in any friendly way. It took me a couple of days, but those verses stayed with me and eventually I asked God for forgiveness and resolved to start to bless Arthur. I have to admit that there was no desire to do it; it was an act of the will and my decision was spurred a little by the end of the verse from Romans quoted above, which stated, *"In doing this you will heap burning coals on his head!"*

Two days later Arthur had a particularly difficult day in the operating room and it was apparent that he would be working right through lunch. I approached him as he sat in the doctors' lounge waiting for the next case. *"Arthur, I thought you might be hungry. I have bought you a sandwich and a Coke."*

His eyes widened momentarily, and then met mine quizzically. *"Thanks very much."*

I smiled and we discussed his difficult morning. A few days afterwards I called him into the ICU to consult him on a case and, as he gave his views, I wrote his suggestions down as orders. I suggested we try to find a mutual time where we could regularly discuss the patients together. Then I invited him to lunch and learned about his family. His wife was pregnant with their third child and he was worried because there were a few problems. He was eager to talk about them.

As I got to know him, an unexpected thing happened. I changed. I developed a growing affection for him as I discovered an unpolished diamond under that rough exterior. He had not had an easy upbringing but had risen above it. His abrasive exterior had seen him through tough times when he had had to rely solely on his own strength, but deep down there was a soft, caring heart that was longing for expression.

Within three weeks we became good friends. I hardly noticed his lack of manners and it seemed as though he had softened in his treatment of the staff. Our operating times became a pleasure, although, of course, there were still moments of disagreement. Like an untamed stallion, he would react with fire to someone who crossed his path, but we now had the mutual trust to speak into one another's lives and he could be reined in, or, alternatively, he could point out my self-righteousness and I could understand his frustration.

A year later Arthur started becoming tired. Usually full of fire and zeal, he mellowed and seemed not prepared to argue. He also looked thinner. Then we heard the reason. He had developed a mesothelioma, a kind of lung cancer associated with exposure to asbestos. He had spent his childhood in an asbestos mining town. Even with chemotherapy the prognosis was poor. Without a miracle Arthur would be dead in a few months, leaving his young family. He was granted sick leave to be with his family and came to say goodbye to all those in the ICU. We prayed with him, which seemed to touch him deeply.

A week later we heard that Arthur had committed his life to Jesus. How grateful I was that God had spoken to me that morning over a year before, urging me to bless him. I tried to imagine how I would have felt had I continued on my path of trying to destroy or discredit him. Apart from missing the chance of seeing the amazing man that he truly was, I would have missed the chance to show care for him and to see him built up with a commitment to Jesus before he embarked on that long journey into uncharted territory — a journey each one of us must take. In Isaiah we read that God's ways are not our ways and, not only that, they are infinitely higher than ours. (Isa. 55:8-9). How very much higher it proved to be to bless when all that was in me wanted to curse. What life it brought, not only to our relationship, but to Arthur as he faced death.

"'For my thoughts are not your thoughts, neither are your ways my ways,' declares the Lord. 'As the heavens are higher than the earth, so are my ways higher than your ways and my thoughts than your thoughts." (Isa. 55:8-9)

Chapter Sixteen

"A HIGH-RISK OPERATION and GOD'S SPECIAL AGENDA

"I pray also that the eyes of your hearts may be enlightened in order that you may know the hope to which he has called you, the riches of his glorious inheritance among the saints, and his incomparably great power for us who believe." (Eph. 1:18,19)

Often we are unaware of God guiding us. It is only as we look back that we can trace His hand. However, sometimes He appears to step in from the start and we are left in no doubt that He is sovereignly in charge of what is happening. Such was the case with Marion.

I received a call from Pete, a surgical colleague and friend. He had a high-risk patient in his rooms and asked if I could come down and give an opinion about giving her an anaesthetic. I went down and met the patient, a thin, anxious lady in her late seventies. She was sitting bolt upright in a chair and gave a brief, nervous smile as I entered. I could tell from her rapid, short breathing and by observing that her chest hardly moved, that she had severe emphysema. This disease causes the lungs to lose their elastic properties so that they can no longer draw in air and then expel it. Marion spent her life struggling to breathe. Even the slightest amount of exercise would leave her panting and breathless. The main arteries supplying blood to her legs had previously clogged and she had had Teflon tubular grafts inserted to carry the blood. The graft to her right leg had now become infected, giving her pain, and threatening the blood supply to the leg. Pete needed to replace it, but Marion's lung condition was now so much worse than when she had originally had the graft, that he was not sure if she would withstand the operation.

After examining her, I felt confident that the operation could be performed reasonably safely under an epidural anaesthetic. That way Marion would be numb in the area of the operation, but would not be asleep and her lungs would be only minimally affected. I asked Pete if he would book her in to hospital a few days early so that she could receive chest physiotherapy and medication prior to the operation. She looked frail and frightened and I found myself inexplicably warming to her. I made up my mind that at the first opportunity I would tell her of God's faithfulness and pray with her.

I attended a prayer meeting the next evening and the power of God was especially evident. At the end one of the ladies called me aside. *"There is a lovely person in our bowling club who is going in for an operation,"* she said. *"Won't you please look her up when she is admitted and say a prayer with her?"* When she told me the lady's name, I told her that I would be giving her anaesthetic and that I had already made up my mind to pray with her. It was Marion.

The day came for her admission and at the end of my operating session for that day I went to visit her, although it was still three days before her operation. I chatted with her and tried to make her feel at ease. Then I told her that I was a committed Christian and had seen how very faithful God was in looking after us when we placed ourselves in His hands. She gave an anxious, startled look and said, *"But I am a Catholic!"*

People say such funny things when they are nervous and out of their normal environment! I assured her that God looks at our heart. It doesn't matter whether we are Catholic, Anglican, Free Church, or anything else. If we ask Jesus to come in and be with us and entrust our life to Him, that is what He died to accomplish. Marion was reassured and I prayed with her. It seemed as if God was just waiting for that moment. Like something tangible, a wave of peace entered my heart and stilled every tension from a busy day. There was no coming gradually into His presence as I experience so often. He just came. I wondered if Marion had felt what I had. As I opened my eyes, it was apparent that she had. She had a look of suppressed joy and kept thanking me. I told her to thank Jesus and keep praying.

The next day I was very busy and did not have time to see her, but the following day I went to see her to examine her before her operation. As I came to her, she scolded me for not seeing her the previous day and, before I could even examine her, said, *"Let's pray!"* Again, God's presence was tangible.

She came to the operating room with no hint of nervousness and, since her operation was done under an epidural, she was awake and we talked throughout the procedure. I kept her in the ICU for the next two days and she did well. The surgeon, however, was not happy. The infection had extended further than he had thought, and he was worried that there was residual infection there. She was discharged to the general ward, but in the days that followed it was apparent that the new graft had now become infected. It would take a major abdominal operation to repair it and, with the state of her lungs, she would probably not survive it. Marion understood the situation and did not want any further surgery. She was at peace and, if she were to die, she wanted to go with dignity, not attached to a ventilator, her body invaded with tubes and pipes, as would be the likely outcome from a further operation. I continued to visit her and to pray with her, but in the next few days she became less and less conscious and she was moved into a side ward. Her sisters were asked to come from England.

I admit I was disappointed, although deep down I knew that Marion's quality of life had not been very good before the operation. I felt as if God had let us down after taking her so smoothly through high-risk anaesthesia and surgery. Everything had gone so well, but in the end, she was not going to make it.

Then a few days later, as I was praying with her, I experienced something that has lived with me to this day, but which is so hard to put into words. She was still conscious, but very sleepy. I was with her in deep prayer, lifting her in my spirit to the throne room of God. Suddenly it seemed the room was filled with light. It was as if Jesus was physically present, and He started speaking to her through me. Although I was speaking, no words were being formed in my mind. I was actually listening as an awed spectator. The words came from Jesus, but out of my mouth. He spoke of His love for her and His power over all things; He spoke words of His pleasure in

84

Marion, of how He had longed to be close to her as He now was. I cannot remember all that He said, but I remember the sense of His presence as if it were yesterday. One could feel the peace that filled that side room as something physical. I do not know how long He was there. Time stood still. At the end I came to myself humbled, awestruck and filled with a deep bubbling, quiet joy. Marion gave a sigh and fell into a deep sleep. With that I left the room.

Marion died two days later, but the peace remained in that side room and continued for about two days afterwards. All the nurses felt it. Marion's sisters came out from England the day before she died. They too felt the peace when they went into the room. They commented that it was the most remarkable experience of their lives.

Why should God have singled Marion out to manifest Himself in such a special way right from the start in order to welcome her home without fear? Why does He not do it more often? These are mysteries that we will only know on the other side of the grave when we, who know Him, will have the wonder of seeing Him face-to-face.

Whenever I read the glorious Scriptures that speak of that moment, I sense, after that experience with Marion, that I have had a tiny glimpse of what is ahead. For most of us, when we die, the door opens and we enter His manifest presence. For Marion it seems that He opened the door and came through to fetch her.

"We believe that Jesus died and rose again, and so we believe that God will bring with Jesus those who have fallen asleep in him." (1 Thess. 4:14)

Chapter Seventeen

TRUSTING GOD in the DARKNESS: A SISTER'S HEARTBREAK

"Trust in the Lord with all your heart, and lean not on your own understanding; in all your
ways acknowledge him, and he will direct your paths." (Prov. 3:5-6)

When Janice joined the ICU nursing team no one had an idea of her background, but she had an aura of deep spiritual quietness that I have come to associate with someone who has suffered much. Although she laughed a lot as she went about her caring work, there was a seriousness and a quiet strength about her, like a deep pool that maintains its stillness even when the surface is ruffled. It is in people like Janice that I see the outworking of what Jesus told a suffering Paul, *"When you are weak, then I am strong."* (2 Cor. 12:9-10)

No one knew just what was happening at Janice's home. We knew that her husband was often out of work and that they and their four children were often solely dependent on her salary. She was intensely loyal, however, and it was only by little unspoken messages (a long silence when someone spoke of their caring husband, polite refusals to invitations to attend events that would cost money, a catch in the voice when speaking of having to leave her children to work overtime), that we knew things were tough. Then, one day, I came into the ICU to see all the girls crowded around her with an air of excitement. Janice had discovered that she was pregnant. As she spoke, it was evident that this pregnancy was unplanned, and she was anxious about how she and her husband would cope financially with a fifth child. Her overall reaction, however, was excitement at the new life forming inside her – an excitement that grew as she felt her baby start to move. She would trust God with her provision when the time arrived.

Then, with the baby just five-and-a-half months old in her womb, she uncharacteristically trudged wearily into the ICU on her day off duty. Her face was strained and her cheeks were streaked with tears as she slumped down in the sisters' office. Concerned staff gathered around her, but it took some time before she could tell us what the matter was. Then it came out with a rush.

"I have just been for a routine ultrasound scan and my baby boy is grossly abnormal." The tears came freely now. *"The doctors said he would probably live for one or two years at the most and that his mental function would be minimal."*

With a voice low with sorrow and confusion, she related the rest of the story.

The doctors had suggested that it would be kinder to abort the baby. It would be very difficult for her to carry it around for another four months, they said, knowing she was carrying a child who would never function fully and who would die early. After birth he would require huge resources in time and money, for possibly one or two years, before he succumbed.

It shocked us all. How do you comfort someone in that predicament? How do you even pray? There were so many questions and no answers. It seemed trite to say that God

87

loved her and she must trust Him. Where was God, anyway? I felt a little alienated from Him in the next few days. Janice had trusted Him for so much and now she had this – the prospect of a little life that, before he died, would drain all their meagre finances and demand all their attention. And what of the other four children? They could not be neglected. The temptation to take the doctors' suggestion and have an abortion was very real. In view of the

huge implications of going to full term carrying an abnormal child, it seemed a "sensible" option. No one could advise her. We all had differing views, anyway. After the initial shock, I turned back to God in prayer. What else was there to do?

Babbie Mason sings a song, the lyrics of which pointed the only way forward. She sings:

"God is too wise to be mistaken,
God is too good to be unkind.
So when you don't understand,
When you don't see His plan,
When you can't trace His hand,
Trust His heart."

We could not understand, and so we had to lean on His character. We had to look back on His faithfulness in dealing with us in the past and, ultimately, to His love expressed so eloquently in dying for us on the Cross.

For the next two months, as Janice came on duty, she regained her composure. If anything, that deep pool got deeper, although she didn't laugh as much. After much prayer and heartache, she decided that she could not kill her baby, though his life would be so short, and refused the doctor's insistent pleas that she have an abortion. It would be the biggest test of her trust in God, but she could not do something that she knew He would disapprove of.

In the second-last month of her pregnancy, Janice left work and the family moved to another town so she could be with her mother. We kept in touch, however, and were anxiously waiting for the due date.

The news came through two weeks before she was due. Labour had been induced and she had delivered her tiny son. He was very weak when he was born, and she held him for two hours before his brand-new life slipped away. She was holding him, kissing him, and expressing her love as he rested with his mom and then, with a sigh, was resting with Jesus. The sister who phoned her said that she had never heard such a sad voice in anyone, but I knew that all the ingredients were there for healing.

Janice had trusted in God throughout:
"The Lord's unfailing love surrounds the (wo)man who trusts in him" (Ps. 32:10)
"How great is your goodness which you have stored up for those who fear you, which you bestow in the sight of men on those who take refuge in you." (Ps. 31:19)

She had refused to stray from His path and have an abortion.
"The eyes of the Lord are on the righteous and His ears are attentive to their cry." (Ps. 34:15)

She had chosen to mourn rather than to take the easy way out:

"Blessed are they that mourn, for they will be comforted." (Matt. 5:4)

She had loved her baby though it broke her heart. She had not rejected him.

"The Lord is close to the broken-hearted and saves those who are crushed in spirit." (Ps. 34:18)

Though I still do not understand why Janice had to go through what she did, once she had chosen the right way, God gave her the grace to go through it.

So often those who choose to abort their babies find that it is not really an easy way out. The effects of that choice can often lead to untold heartache and guilt feelings later.

Because of what she went through, and the way that she chose to go through it, I felt sure that Janice had been given a unique opportunity to bring healing to other bereaved mothers and those contemplating abortion.

"Praise be to the God of all comfort, who comforts us in our trouble so that we can comfort others with the comfort we, ourselves, have received." (2 Cor. 1:3,4)

Chapter Eighteen

RELOCATION

"In his heart a man plans his course, but the Lord determines his steps." (Prov. 16:9)

The year was 1995. I had been in practice in Pietermaritzburg for 21 years and praying with my patients for 17 of those years.

Those were heady days in South Africa. We had just witnessed the astounding mercy of God as Nelson Mandela was released from prison and Black leaders sat together with their former White oppressors in a Constitutional Committee and planned a Constitution for a new, democratic South Africa. As we moved towards the first truly universal election, we were the object of a huge global outpouring of prayer. What had started as apprehension turned into euphoria as the day approached? The scenes relayed across the world of orderly, joyful queues snaking back kilometres from the polling stations have become one of the wonders of world history. Reporters who were on hand to film the guns and bombs, instead reported excited old men and women waiting for hours to cast the first vote in their long lives, and White

91

and Black people sharing stories and meals as they waited patiently side by side to vote.

We had been a democratic South Africa for less than a year when God sent my life in a different direction. …

The telephone rang loudly, breaking into my thoughts as I pored over the operating list for the following day. It was a Sunday afternoon and I was in our deserted office, having just finished an appendicectomy at St. Anne's Hospital nearby. Since I was in the area, I had popped in to see what was in store for me the next day. The telephone's ring puzzled me. Who would be phoning the rooms on a Sunday afternoon? Surely they would not expect anyone to be here. I debated for a moment as to whether I should answer it or not but moved into the secretaries' office and picked it up.

"Hello."

A lady's voice with an Irish accent responded.

"Hello, I am looking for Dr David Walker."

This was remarkable. I had walked in there two minutes before and would only have been there for another five minutes. Out of eleven partners I was the one who had been operating at St. Anne's and who had, on impulse, decided to come to the rooms. I would not normally have picked up the phone under such circumstances, but I did. Who could it be?

"Dr Walker speaking."

"This is Bridget, from Tawam Hospital. I would like to fax through an application form for employment for you to complete."

That was when I knew that God was opening new doors for me. For some time I had been feeling inexplicably uneasy. I had moved back into private practice after a spell working for the State and things were going well. I was seeing God move in wonderful ways, bringing comfort, peace and healing

92

through prayer, but my spirit was restless, as if there was something that needed to be put right between me and God, but I had no idea what it was. I had sought His face in prayer but had received no answer.

Then one of my partners, who had left the practice to move to the Middle East, invited me to join his hospital there. I had completed a month's locum as a trial and loved it, but I wanted to hear clearly from God that this was where He wanted me to be. All the coincidences that placed me in my rooms as that telephone rang convinced me. He wanted me in the United Arab Emirates.

Thus, in 1996, I found myself speeding through the desert on a three-lane highway lined with trees, each one drip-fed with desalinated water, on my way to a new post in an ultramodern hospital for the local population.

I immediately felt at home in Arabia. It was as if I had stepped into the pages of the Bible, especially those of the Old Testament. Everything that it spoke of was contemporary. The camels and the sheep of the Bible's pages came alive in context as I saw them wandering through the desert, feeding from the sparse bush, and drinking from water drawn from wells. The streams in the desert, cascading through wadis, crystalline and cold, could be visited after hours of arduous driving through parched, barren wasteland scorched by an unrelenting sun. The kings of the Bible, with their many wives and favourite sons had their contemporary counterparts in the Sheikhs. Even the Pharisees of Jesus' day who sought a righteousness of their own through keeping the Law, had their equivalents in the rigid adherence of the local population to the strict laws of Islam. As I read my Bible there was no need to transpose the context into another time zone. It was all around me.

And the barrenness of the desert has a simple, uncluttered beauty that feeds the soul like no other. Not assailed by sensory overload, the spirit is free to be still, to meditate and hear the whisper of God.

Twenty-five years before I arrived, the United Arab Emirates was a conglomeration of tribal sheikhdoms, known as the Trucial States, with each Sheikh having absolute power over his little domain. Wilfred Thesiger, the renowned explorer of Africa and Arabia, vividly describes warring tribes that are clearly reminiscent of the descriptions in the Bible of Abraham's life in Canaan (see Genesis 14:1-17). A sobering reminder of just how similar they were to Biblical times came to me one day when I started my ward round of the ICU.

The Medical Officer was giving a summary of the night's admissions. He described a very old man who had been admitted in a state of serious neglect. He had severe malnutrition, dehydration and hypothermia (a critically low temperature). As I entered his ward, I inwardly recoiled at what I saw. In the bed huddled an emaciated old man whose bones, protruding from every prominence, were covered only with fragile, dry skin. What riveted my attention, however, was his face. Where his eyes should have been were empty cavernous sockets, making his emaciated face look like a living skull.

"What happened to his eyes?" I asked, still incredulous at the sight before me. The nurse told me the story.

Over 50 years ago he had been the proud leader of a sheikhdom in Oman. A neighbouring tribe wanted to form an alliance with him against some of the other sheikhdoms. He refused, however, so the neighbouring sheikh laid siege to his city. After many weeks, the city was taken and, just as

94

Nebuchadnezzar had done to Zedekiah 2500 years before, as the penalty for resisting, his eyes were gouged out.

The Trucial states had this advantage over those of Abraham's time, however. As a British protectorate they were protected from foreign interference, by the British Army. Then in 1971, with a federal Constitution having been agreed upon, Britain withdrew its armed forces and the Trucial States gained independence as The United Arab Emirates (UAE), under the presidency of Sheikh Zayed bin Sultan Al Nahyan. The longer I lived in the UAE the more I appreciated the genius and vision of the President. In twenty-five years he had established state-of-the-art communications, transport, health, and education systems, using the wealth of the country to uplift its citizens. He also used the enormous wealth generated by oil to initiate ambitious conservation projects. His work for the preservation of the Arabian Oryx and the sand gazelle earned him the prestigious Gold Panda Award from the World Wildlife Fund. Vast areas of desert land were being reforested, each tree drip-fed by water desalinated in Abu Dhabi and pumped into the region.

During our time there, Sheikh Zayed bin Sultan Al Nahyan became frail and ill, and one member of our Anaesthetic Department was seconded to be on duty at the palace at all times. We were required to be ready, should he collapse, to resuscitate him.

When he was driven anywhere, we were to follow closely behind him in a car packed with resuscitation gear. One day I was in the car with the royal physician, following, at breakneck speed, the black Mercedes of the President, when it suddenly turned off the highway onto a good desert road. We hardly reduced speed as we careered past huge sand

95

dunes pockmarked now and then with a scrubby tree or tuft of grass.

Suddenly the scenery changed. The dunes had been flattened; structures that looked like pumping stations peered above the ground and, like a scraggly army in battle formation, a million little trees barely a metre tall stood in line upon line stretching to the horizon. Each tree was drip-fed from piping that traversed the rows and caused a damp patch at each tree's base. It was forestation on a massive scale. After a few kilometres we were back amongst the dunes. Then unexpectedly, in the middle of the desert, we slowed down as we drove past a hedge of flowering shrubs and trees. Then we turned through a massive, ornate, white gateway. There stretching before us, lay a red road. On either side of us trees, shrubs, lush lawns, and the song of birds transformed this oasis in the desert into a secluded paradise. Like a red carpet five hundred metres long the road led to a pristine, white palace that shimmered before us from its position on a man-made hill that was tiled in its entirety. I felt as if I had been transported into a fairy tale, so extraordinary was the scene before me. I learned later that this was the twenty-fifth desert palace to have been built by the President. It was nearing completion and he had come to check on its progress.

It was in this atmosphere of living in a culture that was so different and fascinating that I saw God at work. I grew to love the Arab people. There is a certain arrogance that develops in an individual of any culture when he has enormous wealth, but underneath is an indefinable vulnerability and a quick recognition of, and appreciation for, authenticity. In talking to the Arab people, one does not have to persuade them of the existence of God. Unlike the

96

secular West, where the starting point is whether God exists, the vocabulary of the Arabs is peppered with references to God. *"Insha'Allah"* (meaning *"If God wills"*), is a natural response to almost every statement. Thus, the starting point is more on the nature of God.

It was not as easy to pray with my patients in the United Arab Emirates. I needed an interpreter to speak to most of them and it was a little harder to gain their trust in a short time. Nevertheless, as the following chapters show, all God is looking for is obedience, a heart for Him and a heart for the people. He then can enter our situations to show His love and to reveal His character. We cannot predict when or how He will act. We can only retain our passion for Him and be faithful to the whisper of His Spirit.

"Dear friends, let us love one another, because love comes from God. Everyone who loves has been born of God and knows God." (1 John 4:7)

Chapter Nineteen

A PUZZLING ILLNESS PRAYER as a WITNESS

"And I have other sheep who are not of this sheep pen. I must bring them also. They, too, will listen to my voice, and there shall be one flock and one Shepherd." (John 10:16)

It is a desperately helpless feeling to see someone critically ill but to not know what the problem is. Such was the case with Fatima, a 50- year-old Egyptian lady. As she lay on the ICU bed, her large, corpulent body, sweating and flushed with fever, heaved with every laboured breath. Her heart was racing and her pulse, full and bounding, shook her body with a tremulous shudder with every heartbeat. She appeared to be in septic shock, but what was the cause? She had a painful abdomen but on examination there was little to find. X-rays, ultrasound, and a CT scan had all been negative.

Quickly, we worked to resuscitate her. First, she needed sedation, a tube in her windpipe and assistance with her breathing. Then all our monitoring lines: one through a vein into her heart to measure the pressure there; another into an artery for continuous blood pressure readings; a catheter in her bladder to check her kidney function; a pulse oximeter on her finger, continuously measuring the oxygen in her blood; and then antibiotics and an infusion of adrenaline.

For an intensivist, there is great satisfaction in all the instrumentation and monitoring that is part of the work. To approach a patient and, like a pilot checking the state of his flight, look at the instruments and see at a glance the state of the patient's heart, lungs, and kidneys gives one an illusion of absolute control. But it is an illusion. Like the weatherman reading the signs and telling us what the weather will be, but with no control over it, the intensivist, too, is just reading the signs. There are so many variables from there on; the choice of treatment, the virulence of the disease, the resilience of the patient, the functioning of the machines and the side-effects of any management. They all emphasize that we are constantly dependent on a caring, powerful God who is waiting to respond to our prayers.

The surgeons and I felt anything but in control of Fatima's condition. She was not improving. The surgeons thought that the problem might be in her abdomen, but they were reluctant to subject someone so unwell to a major operation without a definite diagnosis. The stress of an operation would certainly make her worse. After three days of vacillation, with Fatima still desperately ill, they decided they must operate. They would need to take an exploratory look into her abdomen to determine and, if possible, rectify the cause. It was particularly hazardous. Fatima's size, her shocked state, and the drugs she was receiving to keep her blood pressure normal meant that she would be very unstable under the anaesthetic. On starting the anaesthetic wild fluctuations in her blood pressure and heart rate kept me constantly checking, adjusting fluids, administering drugs, checking again. Like a walk on a tightrope, it was a balancing act, titrating the anaesthetic. A

99

little too much and her blood pressure plummeted. Too little and she could regain consciousness. So it was particularly disappointing that no cause for her condition was found at surgery. As we finished the operation and wheeled her back to the ICU she was in a parlous state and unlikely to survive.

Her husband, Magdi, had kept away prior to the operation, watching apprehensively from a distance as his wife was subjected to the alien electronic world of bouncing screen traces and bleeps and alarms and needles and tubes and bellows. But now he was by my side, fidgeting absent-mindedly with his prayer beads as he listened to the bad news. We could find no cause for his wife's predicament. It was likely to progress and the operation had made it worse.

For the next 48 hours Fatima lay precariously between life and death. Morning and evening Magdi, his face pale and jaw tense, would come through and ask me stiffly if there was any progress. Each day I had the same reply, *"No change."*

On the evening of the second day, as I was attending to her, with Magdi hovering anxiously nearby, still fingering his prayer beads and with extracts from the Qur'an scattered on her bed, I sensed that I should openly lay hands on Fatima and pray for her. I suggested this to Magdi, but he pretended not to hear. Still, I sensed an urging in my spirit to pray. Again, I suggested it and again he acted as if he had not heard me. Finally I said, *"I would really like to pray for your wife and ask my God to heal her,"* and, without waiting for any response from him, I laid hands on her and asked God, in the name of Jesus, to heal her.

As I walked away, I felt an exhilarating lightness in my spirit and a definite whisper from God, "She is healed!" Sure enough, by that evening she had improved considerably. The next morning, a strained and tense husband asked me how she was. As I told him that she had improved markedly, I was unprepared for the reaction. He threw his arms around me and kissed me profusely on my neck and cheeks. Hot and flustered, struggling to regain composure at this distinctly Egyptian (and far from Western), response, I managed to stammer that God is good and that Magdi must now try to get some rest. He said he would, but *"Was I going to pray some more?"* I assured him that I was.

Fatima improved daily, though we never knew what had caused her illness. Every morning, as I entered the ICU, Magdi was waiting at the door with the same question, *"Are you going to pray?"* and a visible sigh of relief when I said that I was.

Within a week Fatima was discharged from the ICU and she continued to make good progress in the ward. We never discovered the cause of her illness. Unfortunately, my schedule did not allow me to see them again. I had to rest content that I was a witness in a chain of events that the Lord had prepared to make Himself known to that special couple from Egypt. God keeps us humble, sometimes, by not allowing us to see the end of His plan. However, so Spirit-led was the encounter, that I have no doubt that He who began the good work in them will be faithful to complete it.

"Being confident of this, that he who began a good work in you will carry it on to completion until the day of Christ Jesus." (Phil. 1:6)

Chapter Twenty

A LITTLE BOY with LEUKAEMIA: PRAYER as a WITNESS

"And you will be my witnesses both in Jerusalem and in all Judea and Samaria, and to the ends of the earth." (Acts 1:8)

Prince was a small eleven-year-old Indian boy who lived with his parents and younger sister in the United Arab Emirates. The family were deeply committed Christians who were now facing a powerful testing. Prince had developed leukaemia and was receiving chemotherapy.

Chemotherapy poisons rapidly-dividing cells. Cancer cells divide rapidly, but there are other cells in the body that divide quickly so these are also affected by the drugs. Hair follicle cells are some of those, so one's hair falls out with treatment. The cells that produce blood, which is formed in the bone marrow, are also poisoned by chemotherapy, thus lowering the immune system. Patients on chemotherapy are very susceptible to infection.

In his third week of treatment, Prince became breathless. Within a day he was unconscious, flushed and shocked. He was rushed into the ICU, attached to a ventilator, and resuscitated. It did not look good. All tests indicated that he was severely immune- compromised and had now developed septicaemia, a blood infection. Within a day he was fighting for his life and losing the fight. Miraculously, though, he rallied. His blood pressure stabilised and he did not die immediately. Nevertheless, the situation remained dire. The septicaemia came from pneumonia and now, with the shock and the infection, Prince had developed a condition called Respiratory Distress Syndrome. I had never seen a case as severe as his. His lungs hardly moved as the ventilator strained to force oxygen into lungs solid with fluid, infection and collapsed air sacs. His blood oxygen levels, as indicated by a pulse oximeter and occasional blood samples, were dangerously low. In fact, those tests merely confirmed what was obvious from the blue- black tinge of his lips and tongue.

Prince's parents worked for a Christian organisation and they mobilized everyone, from India to the Middle East, to pray for Prince. Yet Prince slowly deteriorated. After two weeks, he was still being ventilated on

100% oxygen with maximum pressures, and still his lips and tongue remained blue.

It is naturally assumed, because it is a first resort in

treating people for a variety of conditions, that oxygen is good for you. While this is usually true, oxygen in high concentrations for prolonged periods becomes a poison. It paralyses enzyme systems and blocks the very healing processes that it enhances in lower concentrations. The lungs become stiffer and more difficult to ventilate, and other organs may also start to fail. Prince had been on 100% oxygen for nearly two weeks. I was meeting his parents in the ICU daily and we were praying for Prince. Then one day, as we were praying, we heard the pulse oximeter change tone very slightly. His oxygen had improved marginally. However, by all medical assessments it was impossible that he would survive.

Donny, the Head Nurse of ICU, was an Australian with a gruff take-it-or-leave-it attitude that belied a deeply caring nature. He was concerned that Prince's parents were placing unrealistic expectations on a marginal improvement which, by medical standards, was negligible. He thought that the parents were not prepared for the inevitable and that, when Prince died, they would be devastated.

"You must understand," he said repeatedly, as he took the parents aside, *"Prince cannot survive. You must prepare for the reality."*

With a shy smile and a characteristically Indian little shake of the head, the father would reply, *"God is good".*

Day after day, Donny repeated his concern that the parents were not preparing themselves for the inevitable. Each time the father's response was the same. *"God is good."*

Constantly through his battle, Prince was bathed in prayer. People from the Christian organisation popped in and always, while there, they prayed. The parents prayed with him during their visits and I joined them when I could. The Muslim staff was present as we lifted him to the Throne of Grace, calling out in the Name of Jesus. The news spread throughout the hospital.

"The Christians are praying for a little boy in ICU."

And all the time Prince was fighting desperately for his life. He developed serious complications. Repeatedly, the ventilator pressure ruptured his weakened lungs and he nearly died as they collapsed. With his lowered immune system there was a constant battle against one infection after the other.

He needed blood transfusions again and again as the infection and the after-effects of the chemotherapy combined to stop any production of blood by his little body. Yet he survived each event. And the hospital was watching.

"The Christians are praying for Prince."
"Prince is doing badly."
"Now Prince is better."
"The Christians are still praying."

Slowly Prince improved. The infections came under control. We were able to reduce the pressure needed to ventilate him. Then we could reduce the oxygen to safer levels.

Then he could take breaths by himself with some assistance from the ventilator.

Bone marrow tests showed no sign of leukaemia. Finally, a weakened, frail little boy, breathing with no assistance from the ventilator, was discharged from the ICU to the paediatric ward.

Four months later I was standing at the ICU door when a little entourage arrived out of visiting hours. It was Prince, his parents and his sister who had come, on his birthday, to bring some cake to Donny and the nursing staff. Prince looked sturdy and well, like a normal little boy, now twelve years old.

I let them in. As they walked up the corridor, I saw Donny, glaring slightly, walking toward them, ready to confront these people who were entering the ICU out of visiting hours. As he drew closer to them, he scrutinized the intruders. Then realization dawned. This gruff, matter of fact man got down on his haunches, his wide eyes brimming with tears and his arms extended as he exclaimed, "It's Prince!!" What a celebration it was in ICU as the nursing staff crowded around and the father repeated what he had said so often to Donny when Prince was so close to death, *"God is good."*

Donny agreed. *"God is good!"*

The news, of course, was already around the hospital. The nursing staff in the paediatric ward had seen Prince slowly get stronger as he was able to start walking and to hold down good nourishing food. The reports had gone out. *"The little boy the Christians are praying for is getting better."*

Two weeks after Prince visited the ICU, the local Minister of Health came on a ward round, as he did from time to time. He was a short, dumpy, pompous man who enjoyed his status, displaying it by barking out abrupt orders. At that time there were many very ill patients who were not responding well to treatment. As he went from cubicle to cubicle, he heard summaries of the patients' conditions and how many of them were struggling to survive.

At the end of the ward round, preparing to leave, he looked around with a haughty, authoritarian air and issued his verdict. *"Things are not going well,"* he said, and barked his advice. *"You should pray more for your patients!!"*

"Let your light so shine before men that they may see your good deeds and praise your Father in Heaven." (Matt. 5:16)

Chapter Twenty-One

A PRAYER MOVEMENT in a MOSLEM NATION

"Call to me, and I will answer you, and tell you great and
unsearchable things which you do
* not know."* (Jer. 33:3)

When I first arrived in the Middle East I decided that I
would let it be known that I would be in one of the
prefabricated huts in the expatriate compound at six o'clock
every Tuesday morning, praying. I was trusting God to bring
people to join me.

For the first three weeks I was on my own. Then a young
nurse joined me. Within a few months we had a loyal band of
five or six people greeting the morning in united prayer. To
attract more people, we moved the time to the evening, and we
had a regular attendance of about ten.

In the meantime, I had discovered a prayer warrior from
Pakistan. Richard, short and muscular, with direct, clear eyes
shining from a strong, square face topped with thick, black hair,
was a kindred spirit in prayer. Though highly intelligent, he
had not gone to school because he had had to support his
family from an early age so, as an adult, he was illiterate.
However, after having an encounter with Christ he had found
supernaturally that he could read his Bible. For many years it

was the only book he could read, but he was now able to read other material. To be with him was always an adventure. He loved Jesus with a bold passion and, even in a Muslim country, he was never afraid to speak of his faith.

Sometimes Richard came to our villa and sometimes I would visit him in his flimsy wooden room, part of a ramshackle village in the industrial part of town. Although it was draughty and dusty, he was better off than many, whose lodgings were metal containers devoid of windows, which stood in the merciless sun that scorched the air to temperatures above 45° Celsius. Wherever we met, our times of prayer, though often loud and vociferous, were nevertheless times of deep intimacy with God.

Sometimes we met at night on a hill overlooking the lights of the city, where we called on our Father to bless what lay below us. Sometimes we prayer- walked the streets. We also spent many an evening walking through the corridors of the mission hospital, praying unseen for the patients closeted behind closed doors, or openly with the staff. Often, after earnest prayer, Richard would raise himself to his full height, look up to the heavens and, with a grand gesture of finality, clapping his hands together in a bold stroke, exclaim, *"Done!"*

Richard longed to join us for our prayer times in the expatriate compound, so I spoke to the authorities, gaining permission for him to do so. That opened the door for many others to join us, including members of a charismatic Filipino church. The worship was loud, passionate and heartfelt and often, in the hush that followed, one was almost too scared to breathe, so tangible was the presence of God that fell, like a mantle of glory over the place. Our numbers grew and within a few years over 50 people crowded into the small room in joyful celebration.

At that time, several people simultaneously sensed a desire for a prayer meeting involving all the churches and little prayer groups that were scattered throughout the city. One of the churches took the initiative. The resulting prayer meeting, held in their church building, though not attended by all who could have participated, had people weeping, others sharing deeply, repenting of past prejudices. Others were at the same time expressing love and appreciation of the diversity, which they had not realized existed, of the Body of Christ in that city. From a questionnaire asking whether the participants thought we should continue, we received an overwhelming, *"Yes, but in a neutral venue."* Where, in a Muslim country could we find a neutral venue large enough to house all the people who would attend? God provided this in an extraordinary way.

Just across the border in a neighbouring country, and accessible without going through any checkpoints, lay a hotel that was recovering from troubled times. The Muslim owner had had a profound religious experience which left him convinced that he should no longer sell liquor at his hotel or provide any services of a dubious nature. This seriously affected his trade, but he remained adamant, to the despair of his brothers, who had shares in the hotel. Profits plunged until the Christians discovered it. Most Christians were happy for there not to be alcohol served and it became the preferred venue for their events. The owner was delighted as his hotel once again prospered. The manager, a committed Christian, was given a free hand to host gatherings. These were usually low-profile, discrete affairs which passed unnoticed by the other guests. When we approached the manager about the possibility of a gathering of approximately 200 people for worship and prayer, he was uncertain. The owner, however, was magnanimous. The Christians were good customers. They behaved well and they paid on time; and he was curious. He wanted to see how they prayed compared with the Moslems. We could use the ballroom.

I will never forget that night, as the ballroom was filled with chairs, overhead projectors were prepared, the band set up their instruments and microphones were placed strategically for those leading the prayers. Then the people started arriving; Westerners from different European nations and the United States, Indians, Pakistanis, Filipinos, Africans from Ghana, Zimbabwe, South Africa and Nigeria, Egyptians and Lebanese, Australians and New Zealanders, all mingling in a glorious foretaste of the day when all nations will worship at the feet of the King. Curious hotel guests, the ladies in their black abeyas, their faces shielded behind burka masks and the men in their long white dishdashas and turbans, peered in the doors. Some even came and sat at the back for a while.

Then we started praising God. There is always a special blessing when the Body of Christ unites in praise and that night it seemed as if the angels joined us, so joyful and liberating was the worship. After worshiping God, we started intercession. I looked around in excitement and deep satisfaction at about 16 groups of 10 or 12 people filling the room. In each group people of different races were huddled together, their heads bowed in earnest prayer and the air was abuzz with voices calling on God for the nation, its leaders and for the Church. I felt sure there was a huge smile on the face of God as the prayers, like audible incense, rose from each group. It was a remarkable time, conceived and orchestrated by God. Each of us felt that we had been part of something far larger than any plan of man.

Who would have guessed, as our small group met in that prayer hut in the hospital compound some years before, that God

110

would allow us to participate in such a remarkable event in a Moslem nation?

The city-wide prayer meetings continued monthly for the duration of my time there and for long afterwards. Who, this side of eternity, will ever be able to estimate the impact of those meetings on the nation?

"...for my house will be called a house of prayer for all nations." (Isa. 56:7)

Chapter Twenty-Two

A GOD beyond UNDERSTANDING

"For my thoughts are not your thoughts, neither are your ways my ways,' says the Lord." (Isa. 55:8)

Eight-year-old Marinette and her younger brother were excited. Daddy was coming home from work and they were waiting on the pavement to meet him. Suddenly a huge Toyota 4 x 4 careered across the road and mounted the pavement, colliding with Marinette and flinging her to the ground. Her head crashed against the brick paving, spurting blood as she lay unconscious, like a broken doll. The Toyota was driven by the 14-year old son of a Sheikh, who had lost control of the large vehicle. Screaming hysterically, Marinette's brother ran into the house shouting for his mother. Concerned bystanders rushed to the scene. One of them bundled the unconscious, bleeding girl into his car, propped her up on the back seat and rushed her to the hospital. It took twelve minutes to get there.

One of the first principles in rescue and resuscitation is to maintain a patient's airway so that the victim can breathe. As soon as Marinette was sat on the back seat her head lolled forward, obstructing her breathing. For twelve vital minutes her bruised, concussed brain was without oxygen. Once at the hospital this was immediately remedied, but the damage was done. On examination she had no major injuries, but she remained on a ventilator in the ICU, deeply unconscious.

The tragedy shocked us all at the hospital. The Sheikh who had let his young son drive his 4 x 4 on a main road, in a futile attempt to bring recompense, made sure that the young girl received the best treatment. Although the child was Egyptian and should therefore have been treated at the expatriate hospital, he arranged for her to be treated at the state-of-the-art hospital for the local population. So she came to our ICU. I was not working in the ICU at the time but, like everyone, I was moved by the story and popped in occasionally to see how she was. After a week, when there was still no sign of her regaining consciousness and a CT scan revealed brain damage from a lack of oxygen, I went to the parents and offered to pray for their little girl.

Tariq and Layla were Coptic Christians. They were very pleased when I offered to pray for their daughter and they willingly joined in.

Day after day we met in the ICU and laid hands on Marinette and prayed for her. After two weeks she was still unresponsive and not breathing. Then she opened her eyes and looked at us. There was no way of knowing what was going on behind those beautiful brown eyes that stared at us through long lashes. She made no attempt to move or to breathe. Her face remained expressionless though her eyes locked on mine. Each time we entered her private ward she fixed those eyes on us, sometimes for as long as ten minutes before turning them upwards and closing her lids. Her face remained impassive.

I spent many hours praying with her. I could not tell if she understood me, but each day, as she looked at me, I spoke to her of Jesus, close to her, looking after her, wanting to make her well. I told her of His love for her and I invited her to pray with me as I asked Him to come and be part of our lives, praying in a way that a little eight–year-old would understand. Day after day for six months the routine hardly changed. It would be a time of prayer and lifting her to the Throne Room of God, often telling her of her specialness in God's eyes, speaking of His love and His desire to heal. And each day those beautiful eyes gazed straight at me with no way for me to tell if she could understand. Occasionally she would yawn, twist her mouth as if she might have been trying to speak but had no control of her mouth. Then the eyes would turn up and she would drift away. Tariq and Layla came to the ICU whenever they could, and we prayed together. After six months there was no change in her condition. Throughout that time, she needed assistance from a ventilator to breathe and, while she moved her legs occasionally, there was no movement of her arms and hands.

But while there was no change in Marinette during those six months, there was a change in me. God put a taste of His divine love into my heart; a love so profound I would willingly have changed places with her if it took that to heal her. Often, I would be prostrate before God in my living room at home calling out to Him for Marinette.

Though not in charge of her case, I felt uneasy about her medical condition. It is highly unusual for someone in the sort of vegetative state that she was in, not to breathe by themselves, nor to move their arms. After she had been in the ICU for nine months, although not officially her clinical physician, I managed to persuade the authorities to move her to a renowned rehabilitation centre in Germany. Her parents, a nurse and I accompanied her.

Because Marinette was an expatriate, we could not make use of the State's sophisticated air ambulance. We took her on a commercial flight. The airline flattened the seats of the last four rows and we put her stretcher over the flattened seats. I sat beside her, regularly squeezing oxygen from an inflatable bag into her lungs, as the passengers near us looked on, some with compassion, some with detached curiosity. Above the drone of the plane, the bleep … bleep of the monitors registered a regular pulse and a normal oxygen content in her blood – everything normal save a little mind that we could not reach and arms and a diaphragm that would not move. And all the time the haunting brown eyes looking straight at me from the face, in tossed black hair, of a beautiful child; those eyes appearing, apparently, to comprehend briefly and then turning upward to disappear behind closing lids.

Finally, the flight was over and the child was safely delivered into the hands of the team at the rehabilitation centre. Her mother stayed with her and the father and I returned to the United Arab Emirates.

Three days later we received the news that she was breathing by herself, but it proved to be short-lived. She could not make the sustained effort. Then the reason became apparent. A CT of her spine showed that she had developed a syrinx of her spinal cord. This is a fluid filled cavity that can form from scarring after damage to the spine. It causes weakness or paralysis of the hands and arms and, in her case, her diaphragm. After two weeks in the centre there was nothing more that they could do for her and she was transported back. This time she did not come back to our hospital, where she had become an embarrassment. She was a constant reminder

115

to the Sheikh of his folly in allowing his young son to drive his 4 x 4 and she was blocking an ICU bed for an extended period, depriving a member of the local population of that bed.

It was far more difficult for me to travel to the expatriate hospital to see her and to pray with her and I could only manage it once a week. Each time I went, though, I felt the extraordinary love of God wash through me into her.

Marinette remained in the same state for the rest of the time that I was in the United Arab Emirates. Much later, after I had returned to South Africa, I learned that she had died in hospital without any improvement.

The story of Marinette was a source of pain to me for many years. Usually I had seen the hand of God in some way when I prayed. Either there would be healing, or an improvement or a manifestation of His presence. But I saw none of those, save a sense of the extraordinary love of God. I so desired her to be healed. What is more, the hospital community and the family knew that we were praying. It was the talk of the hospital and beyond and I wanted the Lord to show Himself to them as a compassionate, supernatural, healing God. I tried to put the episode behind me, and I focused on other things. After all, I could still give witness to the power and presence of God in many situations. I had seen Him work so wonderfully. …But then the thought would come from nowhere *"But what about Marinette?"* Where was God then?

Several years later, during my quiet time with the Lord, I was reading about forgiveness. I could think of no one to whom I needed to extend forgiveness but I prayed and asked God if there was anyone I should forgive. To my surprise, I thought a heard a whisper in my spirit, *"Yes, My child. You need to forgive Me."* With that came the memory of Marinette.

I write letters to God during my times with Him and also write what I think He is saying to me. The words flowed from my pen as I poured out my heart to Him. Why had He not healed Marinette? Where was His power when so many were watching to see if He would come through? What about the pain of her parents; did He not care about them? As the words flowed, so did my tears, dropping in smudges onto the page. Then, as I opened myself up, my hurt soul naked before the Lord, I felt a wave of love flow over me like a spiritual tsunami. I started to write what I sensed my heavenly Father was saying:

"David, My precious child, you have no idea what your compassion and love for Marinette did in that community. I say in My Word that the people will know that you are Mine by your love. You showed the community what it is like to love with My love. Although Marinette was not healed, you brought her into My Presence with your prayers and love. She felt Me beside her as you prayed. Her parents, too learned how to pray from the heart. Be assured she is with Me healed and happy and I touched many lives positively through that experience."

Suddenly I felt a freedom in my spirit. The episode became one of pleasure, not of pain. Yes, I would love to have seen Marinette healed, but God knew how to use that tragedy to maximum effect for His glory. There was a lesson in this for me. Even when we do not see God at work, He can be working profoundly. We need to trust Him. Mother Teresa once said, *"God has not called me to be successful; He has called me to be faithful."* Our obedience opens the door for God to work, even though we might not see it.

This chapter is as much about my healing as it is about Marinette.

117

If we are honest with God about our pain, He will reveal His love and heal us. As I look back on the times of ministry to Marinette and see, once more, those beautiful eyes locking on mine, I can picture the Holy Spirit ministering, pouring His love into that little spirit, creating an awareness of Jesus and preparing her for her place beside Him. God is beyond understanding but He is not beyond knowing. We can know Him as our loving Father, whether we are a privileged anaesthesiologist, a grieving parent, a compassionate bystander, the reader of this chapter or even a little brain-damaged girl.

"Be still, and know that I am God." (Ps. 46:10)

Chapter Twenty-Three

PENNY – COMING HOME

"The Lord is good, a refuge in times of trouble. He cares for those who trust in him." (Nah 1:7)

My time in the United Arab Emirates was a time of exhilaration as I saw God at work. It was also a time of deep personal trial. Eighteen months after moving to the United Arab Emirates a routine check- up revealed a small lump in Penny's neck. To our shock, a needle biopsy showed that the cancer had returned. Further investigation revealed that it had spread beyond any hope of a permanent cure.

Nevertheless, it was recommended that she have chemotherapy and then radiotherapy. Initially, with the start of chemotherapy, she again plunged into severe depression, enveloped in a dark shroud of isolation and privation. Our eyes are a window to the soul, says the Bible, and all that Penny saw of her present circumstance and the future was as stark and barren as the harsh black mountains of Oman, our neighbouring state that rose burning and menacing two hours' drive away.

She went back to Pietermaritzburg, as was customary for her in the summer, to escape the cauldron of the desert at that time. Like a half- person, negative and despairing, she boarded the plane, not wanting to go, but not wanting to stay. While in Pietermaritzburg, God intervened through her previous oncology sister (whom she had grown to love), and a caring physician. They loved her back to life, breathing hope into a despairing heart and courage into a sagging, staggering spirit.

Only God could have brought about the transformation that came over Penny. She returned as one of the most positive, joyful people that I have ever met. She was always a little unsure of her true worth in Jesus, but, in her humility, seeing herself no better than others, she shone with His love and light in a way that reverberated through any personal encounter, leaving the recipient beaming and uplifted. She waved to the gardeners at the hospital and at first they half-waved back, astonished that anyone should acknowledge them. Then as she waved the next time they would respond enthusiastically. Sometimes she would stop and talk to them and their stance would straighten, heads held high and they would beam.

It was ecstasy and anguish for me. I loved seeing God use her in such an amazing, unusual way and yet I agonised as she became weak and nauseous with the treatment. No one, seeing her gracious, genuine smile and listening to her joking with the workers or sympathising warmly with them would have guessed at the inner strength that she was mustering as her body cried out in fatigue and discomfort. On many occasions she developed septicaemia after her treatment and needed admission to hospital.

On one such occasion she was admitted during a time when the hospital had changed their cleaning company. The new company had recruited girls from Sri Lanka as cleaners, teaching them some basic Arabic before importing them and dumping them in the hospital. Hesitant, frequently

120

terrified and rendered speechless through their poor grasp of the language and callous treatment by some of the local population, they crept around the hospital like wraiths, afraid to be seen for fear of being placed in a situation they could not manage.

Thus it was that Lettie came hesitantly into Penny's ward, to be greeted by a radiant smile and warm welcome. Penny was a cat lover and had a picture beside her bed depicting two fluffy, white kittens at play. While neither patient nor maid spoke the other's language, they managed to hold an animated sign language conversation about the picture, as it became apparent that Lettie was also a cat lover. It became a routine. Each day, as Lettie came in, they would have a brief warm "chat" as she held the picture to her bosom before she started her cleaning.

One day Penny asked me to take the picture and have it duplicated and framed. As Lettie arrived and reached, as usual for the picture on the bedside table, Penny's hand went on her arm to stop her. Lettie glanced fearfully at her. Had she done something wrong? Then Penny reached into her bedside drawer and pulled out Lettie's very own picture. Lettie stood motionless, overcome with emotion and unable to speak. She had never before in her life been given a gift. The following day it was evident that Lettie had told her dormitory mates. During their tea break ten Sri Lankan maids arrived at Penny's ward and started a routine that continued for the duration of her stay. Every day they would give up their tea break to come and stand around her bed, hardly speaking, gazing adoringly at her for ten minutes. Then one by one as they prepared to go back on duty, they filed past her, each of them in turn laying a hand on her head and saying, in broken, heavily-accented English, *"We 'Amen' for you, sister."*

121

After Penny's discharge, Lettie visited her in the Outpatients' Department on her chemotherapy days. Penny bought her a little tape recorder and gave her Gospel messages in Sinhala, the Sri Lankan language. Then Lettie announced that she would come to tea. A week later she arrived, unannounced, at our villa. Penny welcomed her warmly and I witnessed a remarkable conversation with Penny speaking English and Lettie speaking Sinhala, yet both quite happy to talk to one another and interact, looking at all our ornaments and cuddling our fluffy cats. They could not understand each other, but what they were saying was loud and clear. *"This is not about the words; this is about relationship."*

One week later, Lettie arrived for tea again, this time with an entourage of eight of her friends. The next time it was twenty. We invited our pastor's wife, who spoke Sinhala, to come along and she started a Bible Study. This, with growth, soon became a church. Today the Sri Lankan Church is one of the largest churches in the district. And it all started with Penny's unconditional love and a picture of two kittens.

Radiotherapy and chemotherapy slowed the cancer's inevitable spread, but when it was evident in Penny's spine, her hips, and her lungs the doctors advised us to come home to South Africa to spend time with our family.

Penny was ill, I could see that, yet, like an eagle in a powerful thermal, her spirit was still soaring. Though outwardly she was wasting away, inwardly she was renewed by an inner joy that radiated to all she met. She never lost the warmth and friendliness that won the hearts of the underdogs in Arabia and was responsible for starting the Sri Lankan church there.

Once back in South Africa, Penny's gift of relating to the underdog continued unabated. She knew the name and family concerns of the parking attendant at the supermarket; she lifted the spirits of the checkout girl as she smiled as if delighted to have been served by her; she volunteered for Hospice work and was a joy and encouragement to the office staff there. She helped at an animal rescue organization caring for each cat as her own and delighted the staff with her sense of joy and compassion. Almost eccentric in her joy, she insisted on giving the pharmacist a hug when she collected her medicines and puzzled her oncologist with her quirky sense of humour.

"Are you needing a new pair of high heels?" she asked once when she was not responding to medication and giving the oncologist problems as to how to proceed.

"High heels?" She looked nonplussed.

"I'm keeping you on your toes!"

We had a couple from church come to visit for no reason. *"We just want to come and be around Penny,"* they said, stroking her arm. *"We want something of what she has to rub off on us!"*

At home I felt slightly schizophrenic. On the one hand I longed to talk deeply of my feelings about Penny's impending death and to have her share hers, but on the other hand she was enjoying life – abundant life – as never before, which it seemed almost sacrilegious to interrupt. While she accepted that she was going to die, to the extent of choosing her own coffin *("I don't want anything fancy, Dave. It's such a waste!"),* she had discovered the joy of giving herself to others and preferred to live in that.

So I cried out to God for her healing in my quiet times with Him; I ached inwardly as I saw her becoming weak and breathless; I loved expressing my love practically as I took her for blood tests, medication, bone m a r r o w b i o p s i e s a n d chemotherapy a n d I enjoyed being in the wake of a life that was so patently anointed, bringing joy wherever she went in spite of all she was enduring.

No one, interacting with her, would have guessed what I witnessed at home as she became weaker and weaker, staggering to the bathroom and back, sitting on the edge of the bed for ten minutes summoning up the strength to get dressed. On her sixty-fourth birthday all the family celebrated with a high tea at a prominent hotel in Cape Town. The laughter and sheer fun rang out through the hall in a joyous celebration of life as Penny and our three daughters teased and joked and reminisced and the grandchildren joined in the fun. Those watching us would never have discerned that Penny had just three months to live. She was already having oxygen but refused to take it with her that day.

And I was aware of the hand of God protecting her in remarkable ways. Although the cancer had spread to many bones including her spine, hips, and ribs, to her lungs and to her bone marrow, she experienced no fractures and little pain. Also, while in the later stages a *CT* scan revealed large cancerous deposits in her brain, her sparkling, warm, joyous personality remained intact, and the chemotherapy that she was given for palliation (unlike that which she had had before), had few side effects. These were all blessings, easing, a little, a very difficult path.

I felt as if I was living in suspended animation, so entwined was my life with hers. I watched her physically stagger through the day, yet relate to people during that day with a bright, alert spirit. I helped her into bed, even having to turn her during the night, so weak was she becoming. I lay

124

awake at night listening for her breathing to make sure that she was still alive.

Finally, she grew too weak even to swallow or cough and one night I knew she could not last through the following day. At four o'clock in the morning I arose and sat in the lounge praying, my Bible on my knees. Suddenly God enveloped me with His tangible presence. He came as an unseen, all-embracing Person; a loving Father of infinite goodness and love and gentleness. Ever so tenderly, He told me deep in my spirit that He was not going to heal Penny physically, and so great was the peace that encompassed me that I accepted that without misgiving. In deep sorrow, yet bathed in comfort, I opened my Bible and read these words, which I had never seen before:

"All glorious is the princess within her chamber; her gown is interwoven with gold. In embroidered garments she is led to the King." (Ps. 45:13-14)

The next afternoon my princess, with her golden gown of a life that reflected the unconditional love and joy of God and garments of righteousness through the blood of Jesus, was led into the presence of our heavenly King. She lapsed into unconsciousness as we were praying with her. Her breathing became more laboured, then slowly subsided. Then it stopped. Nothing moved. Suddenly she momentarily opened her eyes as if she had seen something. Then she was gone. I believe we had a glimpse of her welcome home.

When we left Arabia to bring Penny back to South Africa, I relinquished most of my anaesthetic activities, particularly in the ICU. It is fitting that my last experience of seeing God work in the setting of critical care should be a personal one, as He ministered so intimately and deeply to me in my time of my wife's critical illness.

The memory of that precious time lives with me today, prompting me to express my love for Him in whatever way I can.

Thank you for walking this journey with me; for reading stories that do not answer the questions that we started with, save with insights into life situations where the chips are down, artificial barriers of race, social status and the like removed, our common humanity exposed and where God has a chance to come through.

The journey started with the death of my brother and anger at a God I did not know or understand and from Whom I alienated myself, and ends with the death of my wife while pressing in close to a God I know, still do not understand, but have chosen to trust and love. In the first instance I found nothing but disquiet and dissatisfaction. In the latter I experienced a love and comfort that made the experience an exquisite anguish.

Nothing can shield us from the unpredictable experiences of a fallen world. How we respond, however, especially to God, will determine how it affects us: whether something in us dies, or whether it springs to a new, fuller more abundant life.

"I have set before you life and death ... Now choose life ... that you may love the Lord your God, listen to his voice and hold fast to him." (Deut. 30:19-20)

Epilogue

"Although the stories of my experiences of God at work in the ICU end here, the story of God's faithfulness and involvement in my life continues.

As I faced the bleakness of life without Penny and the desolate ache in my heart, like a discordant tune, reached crescendos in overflowing tears, I discovered anew the truth that God is close to the broken-hearted and saves those who are crushed in spirit. I do not think that I have ever been so constantly, intimately, in His presence as comfort and pain intertwined throughout each day. It was hard to imagine that it would ever end, but God led me on.

He took me on a journey with a group of American surgeons and anaesthesiologists to Central China where we repaired the clefts in the lips and palates of ninety-nine infants and children. As Westerners we were saying, *"One more and we would have made a hundred,"* till we heard the Chinese saying, *"Ninety-nine is such a lucky number!"* And I learned another lesson. When I was hurting and wanting to turn in on myself, the remedy was to give! Though I thought I had nothing left, as I gave, I found I had more to offer. As I did things God's way, imitating in a tiny way what He did supremely on the Cross, as, in agony, He gave His all, He was honoured and I was blessed.

It was a wonderful, life-giving distraction sitting beside the surgeon in a consulting room in a Chinese hospital as an elderly Chinese peasant, his weathered face creased in a smile, stretched out gnarled hands holding his round-faced, slant-eyed grandson for us to examine; or interacting with expectant, grateful Chinese parents who for the most part were warm and vivacious, quite unlike the 'inscrutable Orientals' of yester-year. And as I took part in a team that turned the deformed lips of infants into pert rosebud mouths, life had meaning once more. There is a special camaraderie within a team that is providing healing for the joy of it with no other reward. Even although the Lord's name may never be mentioned it is the stuff that the Kingdom of God is made of and as such reaps the benefits of the Kingdom.

I heard stories from other trips that had been made, the most touching of which was of a seventy-year- old man who requested that his cleft lip be repaired. When ask why, at his age, he wanted it repaired, with a loving glance at his wrinkled life-time partner beside him, he replied, *I would like to be able to kiss my wife properly.*

We were entertained royally by the authorities with banquets, foot massages, sightseeing, and a karaoke evening. On one occasion the local anaesthesiologists treated us to dinner at an upmarket restaurant. I helped myself to an exotic pasta dish that came past from the rotating centre of the table. As I put it in my mouth, claws and bones and the rubbery texture of bloated skin told me that the 'pasta' was, in fact, chickens' feet. The deep-fried frogs were easy to spot but otherwise one generally had to whisper a quick request for the Lord's blessing on the food and take a lucky dip. For the most part I loved the dishes, although it was an adventure not knowing what was tickling one's palate!

Early in the mornings I took the opportunity to prayer walk around the neighbourhood, interceding for the people as they greeted the day with their morning activities. Their pictures still play back in my mind. Some of these are of a bent old man with a white wisp of beard trailing from the point of his chin sitting outside a hole in the wall selling exotic dried vegetables; a group of younger men noisily playing a card game in a dimly lit, smoke-filled room, slapping the cards down with a swagger and vociferous shouts. Further on, in a garden of green lawns, curving paths and arched bridges, there was a group of twenty or more people exercising in the trance-like, slow motion dance of Tai Chi; while out in the street an old lady with a floppy hat sheltering a leathery face creased with laughter lines was pulling a rickshaw cart laden with vegetables.

Finally, our trip was over, and I came home to an empty house with no one to regale with my experiences. God was still close, however, and as I shared my heart with Him, Scriptures kept popping up in my devotional times.

"Two are better than one," He whispered through His Word. Then, *"A prudent wife is a gift from the Lord."* Then again, *"He who finds a wife finds a good thing."*

After forty years of marriage to Penny I could not imagine myself married again, but true to His Word, He put me together with Margie.

We have adventured back to China, prayer walking and interacting with the village folk. While there, we have had fun travelling on a local bus driven by a hyperactive driver who spent the entire journey up steep, winding mountain passes singing loudly, shouting into his mobile phone and turning and conversing noisily with the Tibetan passengers behind him. We have seen the red-robed Tibetan monks sitting on the riverbanks, their long, trumpeted horns stretching out before them as they sought to placate the river gods with the horns' mournful, hoarse tone.

129

Back home we have had the privilege of befriending the homeless and proclaiming the love of Jesus in word and deed.

A part of me died with Penny's death and still another when my anaesthetic career came to an end, yet in God there is always life. There has been a resurrection with a new wife and a new ministry.

While we are alive and while we are in love with Him the adventure continues.

Glossary

Aneurysm – an abnormal dilatation of an artery, causing it to weaken.

Aorta – the main artery that comes directly from the heart. The 'trunk' of the tree that branches into all the other arteries that supply the body with blood.

Appendicectomy – surgical removal of a patient's appendix.

Arterial – belonging to, or within, an artery.

Artery – a blood vessel that carries blood from the heart to the tissues.

Cardiac – Relating to the heart.

Catheter – a tube used in the body for draining or infusing fluids.

Cautery – burning and coagulation of the bleeding points in a surgical wound, usually by passing an electric current through them.

CPR – cardiopulmonary resuscitation. Resuscitation of a patient who has suffered a cardiac arrest.

Craniofacial – relating to the face and the skull as it affects the face.

Diathermy – the process of passing an electric current through tissue to cauterise it.

Donor – the person whose organ is being donated to another.

ECG – electrocardiogram. A measure of the electrical activity of the heart.

Emphysema – a lung condition, often associated with smoking, that causes the lungs to lose their elastic properties.

Endotracheal tube – a tube that is inserted into the patient's windpipe to breathe for him and to protect the airway from inhaling foreign material.

131

Epidural – Outside the dura, the outermost membrane covering the spinal cord.

Epidural space – a region outside the dura that can readily be filled with fluid.

Epidural anaesthetic – the injection of local anaesthetic into the epidural space, bathing the nerves with local anaesthetic as they emerge from the spinal cord. This is usually done via a catheter which is inserted into the epidural space.

Fracture – a break (referring to a bone).

Graft – a structure that is placed in the body surgically to take the function of a part that has failed to work.

Haemostatic – stopping the flow of blood.

Hypothermia – a critically low temperature usually due to prolonged exposure. It can be fatal.

ICU – Intensive Care Unit.

Intensivist – a doctor who has specialised in Intensive Care work.

Internal jugular vein – the largest vein draining blood from the brain back to the heart.

Intravenous – (IV) - within a vein.

Jaundice – yellow, usually from liver failure.

Laryngoscope – an instrument to assist in placement of a tracheal tube.

Milestones – A child's developmental parameters.

Neurosurgeon – A surgeon who operates on a patient for a condition related to the nervous system.

Neurosurgical – related to surgery involving the nervous system of the patient.

Oedema – the accumulation of fluid in the tissues.

Orthopaedic – relating to the bones. **Pentothal** – an intravenous anaesthetic drug. **Pubis** – the front part of the pelvis.

Pulse oximeter – a device which clips onto the finger and measure the amount of oxygen in the blood.

Radiologist – A doctor who has specialised in all fields related to X-rays.

Recipient – the person receiving the donated organ. **Registrar** – a qualified doctor under specialist training. **Resuscitate** – literally *"to bring back to life"* but used in the context of reviving someone who is close to death. **Septicaemia** – a severe infection of the blood.

Shock – Failure of the circulation, usually with a low blood pressure.

Stent – a rigid tube placed inside an artery to keep it open.

Syrinx – a fluid filled cavity in the spinal cord, usually as the result of an injury to the cord.

Tracheal tube – a tube placed in a patient's windpipe to protect the airway or to provide assistance with breathing.

Trauma – injury, physical or emotional, but used for physical injury in the context of this book.

Vein – a blood vessel that drains blood from the tissues back to the heart.

Vena Cava the largest vein in the body, being the confluence of all the other veins and transporting the blood directly to the heart.

Ventilator – A machine to assist, or take over, the breathing of the patient.

Prayer of Salvation

If, in reading this book, you have realised that you do not have a personal relationship with the God who acted in the stories within these pages, and you desire one, it is just a prayer away. The holy, pure God of the universe has made a way, through *Jesus*, for us to approach Him without having to earn our way through any good deeds. Since *Jesus,* as He went to the Cross, paid the penalty for all the wrong that we have ever done, we need only to come as we are, asking forgiveness, repenting and turning from the things that we know are wrong and requesting Him to come into our lives. The following is a suggested prayer. You need not use it parrot fashion, but as a guide as to what is required, to come from your heart:

"Lord Jesus Christ, please forgive me for the things that I have done wrong in my life (take a few moments to ask forgiveness for anything specific that comes to mind). Thank you that you died on the Cross for me so that I could be forgiven. I receive your forgiveness and ask you to come into my life as my personal Saviour. Come dwell with me and in me by the power of your Holy Spirit. I give my life to you. Amen"

Once you have prayed this prayer from your heart it is important to tell someone, just to consolidate that decision and to underline it when doubts come as to whether you really have done it. It is probably best to tell someone who will be pleased to hear it.

Then you need to find an alive, Bible-believing church to belong to, start to read your Bible daily (there are many Bible reading aids on the web) and talk to God (pray) daily.

Your life will be transformed beyond your dreams. And I would love to hear from you.

About the author

Dave Walker is an anesthesiologist with a special interest in the ICU. He has practiced in South Africa, the diamond mines of Namibia, the United Kingdom, the Middle East, and China.
As a committed Christian, he is passionate about prayer, because he has seen the way God answered as he prayed with his patients, which is mainly what his autobiographies are about.

An adventurer at heart, he has climbed Kilimanjaro twice, hiked part of the Annapurna circuit and all over Zimbabwe and South Africa.

He lives in Howick, KwazuluNatal, South Africa and has three daughters and seven grandchildren.

Email: walkdave5@gmail.com

Facebook: Scribewalker

Web: http://www.scribewalker.com

<u>Dave Walker MD's other books are:</u>

Prayer, Medicine and Miracles.

In his second book, Dave Walker MD takes a closer look at what it means to be a Christian witness, seeing God work both in the hospital and outside its walls, as he visits a shelter for the homeless and prayer walks through a maximum-security prison.

Crisis in the Children's Ward.

Dave Walker MD's novel weaves medical mystery, South African rural pagan religious practices and a solid Christian message into an intriguing story that will keep you guessing till the end.

Listen to the Music and Other Stories.

His latest book is an anthology of short stories, most of which have come within the top five of Faithwriter's Writing Challenge.

Many of them are fiction, or fictionalised accounts of true stories, by which he conveys truths about God and His ways to encourage, challenge or comfort the reader.

Made in the USA
Las Vegas, NV
21 May 2021